Your Self as History

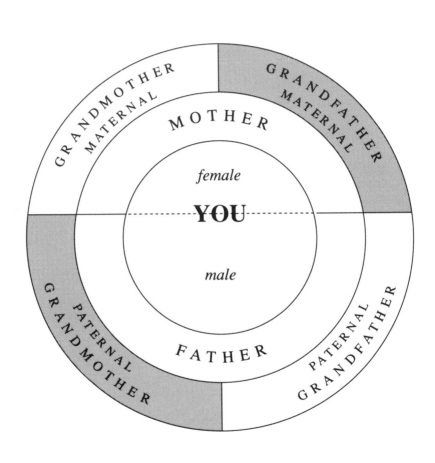

Your Self as History

Tracing Your Past to Enrich Your Future

Valentine Rossilli Winsey

MADISON BOOKS
Lanham • New York • London

Copyright © 1996 by Madison Books

Originally published in 1992 by Pace University Press.

Published by Madison Books
4720 Boston Way
Lanham, Maryland 20706

3 Henrietta Street
London WC2E 8LU, England

Library of Congress Cataloging-in-Publication Data

Winsey, Valentine Rossilli.
Your self as history : tracing your past to enrich your future / Valentine Rossilli Winsey.
p. cm.
1. Family. 2. Personality development. 3. Genealogy. 1. Title.
HQ515.W55   1992   306.85—dc20   92–4698   CIP

ISBN 1-56833-074-X (pbk : alk. paper)

Distributed by National Book Network

⊖™ The paper used in this publication meets the minimum requirements of
American National Standard for Information Sciences—Permanence of
Paper for Printed Library Materials, ANSI Z39.48–1984.
Manufactured in the United States of America.

We all come from the past, and children ought to know what it was that went into their making, to know that life is a braided cord of humanity stretching from time long gone, and that it cannot be defined by the span of a single journey from diaper to shroud.

Russell Baker, *Growing Up*

Contents

Acknowledgements

Wholehearted thanks to my students who, in the course of researching their family histories helped me fashion the parameters set forth herein. And to the following:

Dr. Seymour Hutner for his diffident perspicacities; his wife, Dr. Margarita Silva Hutner for evenings of tea and empathy;

Michelle Fanelli, Head of Readers' Service and Rey P. Racelis, Reference Librarian of the Henry Birnbaum Pace N.Y.C. University Library for their invaluable research assistance;

Blanche Amelkin, Director of Support Services of Pace, her supervisor, Jackie Myers and staff member, Praimatee Mosodeen for their diligence in preparing the manuscript's final draught;

Dr. J. Houle, former dean of faculty of the Dyson School of Arts and Sciences, Pace U., N.Y.C. for his continuous encouragement; Professors Dorothea Von Huene and Barbara Blumberg for testing some of my materials in their classes;

Miss Jeanna Bernkopf, Editor-at-large; Diana Maul, Archivist, Ann Loring, former president of the N.Y. chapter of AFTRA, Professors Sherman Raskin and Mark Hussey for their interest and support and editorial assistance;

And finally, my husband, Aubrey, and daughters Kim and Christina for their forebearance and sense of humor that sustained me during this prolonged effort.

Preface

Few conflicts hurt more than those between generations. They often stem from ignorance about your forebears and how the forces of change have so transformed their physical environments as to effect near-total destruction of their social environments as well. Lacking such knowledge, you cannot accurately assess the almost chaotic-seeming environments in which you find yourself. *Chaotic-seeming* is a fair statement because, after World War II, the explosive expansion of science and technology enabled humans for the first time to stretch the limits of their adaptability from an earth-bound one to even the potentiality of emigrating to colonies in outer space, and to extend the span of satisfactory life.

Ignorance of the lives of your forebears may induce a sense of unduly vague selfhood generating an illiteracy both of self-awareness and of culture. Many among you are becoming aware of this feeling of unrelatedness and discontinuity—one extending beyond yourselves and your forebears, the academic world and—for that matter—the world at large, as well.

Small wonder, then, that now over 500 undergraduate-level courses in family history are being taught around the country. Need grows for guidebooks. This guidebook, accordingly, aims to provide a framework as scientific—i.e., objective—as possible to enable you to research and write your own history along with those of your parents and grandparents. It might help you come to terms with your heritage, while learning how to understand and appreciate it better within the context of the present.

Methods and assignments for this enterprise are suggested here. They have obvious limitations, but may serve to help you attain important objectives in which every researcher engages—that is to say, to:

1. experience the research process first hand;

2. distinguish between primary and secondary sources;

3. learn to ferret out supportive statistical data from the purely descriptive, reportorial, anecdotal, and/or analytical materials;

4. assess such various kinds of data for arriving at conclusions.

For practical reasons the *Family History Guidebook* suggests that research be limited to three generations of your family, counting your own.

A Word for Teachers

Designed as it is to fit the time-constraint of a three point undergraduate course in Family History research, the guidebook offers a fairly well tested approach while mindful of related undergraduate courses, e.g.:

• *Cultural Anthropology:* The study of behavior in different cultures could be made alive to students of such varied backgrounds as Black slaves, Italian peasants and Siberian exiles, making them aware that their classroom is a cultural-anthropological field extension of a sort in itself. In other words, the abstract study of humankind takes life from their own personal, cultural histories.

• *Sociology:* Retrospective study of his/her family which historically has been the basic group may lead the student to grasp the significance of it as a socializing reality vis-a-vis other institutions.

• *Psychology:* The study of theories of personality could show how the family fosters (or not) personal development. By learning to regard parents and other relatives as individuals in their own right, the student may better grasp the concepts dealt with in this course.

• *American History:* This study may enable the student to sense how history is written—the uncertainties, even pain—as she/he sifts primary and secondary sources and strives, despite gaps, to shape a coherent story. For her/him history then becomes more than a chronicle of far-off events bestrewn with epic characters.

• *English:* a colleague on the Pace faculty (English Department) similarly assigns work in her course, *The American Scene,* in which students note how the sort of information they are gathering about themselves has served writers of stories and biographies.

This is an initial effort. The methods outlined are intended to encourage flexibility in student thinking, yet center on the theme of bettering their understanding of their position within their own family. This, in turn, should enable them to cope more effectively with their daily problems and understand their origins in the family and the specific American scene.

Preparation of this book has been encouraged by past students. I've received encouragement also, from teachers; several have already used it.

I've been developing this guidebook for 10 years. It has generated much interest. In 1981 I was invited with three of my students to a conference at Syracuse University on the family. I presented a paper and the students participated in a panel discussion. The resultant article appeared in *Anthropology and Humanism Quarterly* (Vol. 7, No. 1, March 1982). At a Pace University–sponsored conference in March, 1984, on the *Multi-Ethnic City: Issues and Opportunities For Educators,* I had many requests for my modus operandi. This made me realize that there was a need for a guidebook like this one. To my knowledge the methods outlined have not been explicitly employed in any collegiate institution in the United States. This is a first edition. I welcome suggestions for improving the guidebook.

Chapter One

Who Am I?

Who am I?
Do I really know?
Am I what I seem to be?

I can swim and fly,
Does that make me
A fish or a bird
Or both? Or neither?

In how many ways
Can I see
Me?

Almost from birth the question—Who am I?—challenges. It begins with awareness of others who, along with parents, siblings, relatives, peers, teachers and acquaintances, sharpen one's sense of self. You may find yourself labeled, "cute", "stubborn", "bright", "clumsy", "outgoing", or "lazy". Abraham Lincoln's family and neighbors consistently referred to him as a good boy who wasn't exactly lazy, "but his mind was often on books to the neglect of work." Such opinions reveal how people see you. But how do you regard yourself? Wrote Margaret Mead in *Male and Female:* "A growing child encounters not only the changes in his own feelings; his feelings about himself and other human beings, but also the feelings which these other humans, especially his parents have about him."

How parents feel about themselves has obviously been influenced in childhood by feelings expressed by their parents. All were born into

1

cultures with their own traditions, history, technological change, style of entertainment, norms of behavior, social structures and institutions.

Of all institutions the oldest and most essential for human survival is the family—the first group into which you were born. From it you have acquired, besides genetically blueprinted attributes, a particular language, mode of expression, mannerisms, attitudes, beliefs, behavior—in short, a heritage that may have decisively shaped your personality. Delving therefore into your family history might help you better understand yourself and appreciate how changes in communications, education, travel, work, environment, play, etc., have also altered the social environment. For example, had you been born a Black woman in the South in your great-grandparents' time, your perception of self, the life choices open to you and your place in society might have been sharply different from how it is today.

A Black student who had regarded slavery simply as a remote institution to be relegated to dusty history books discovered that a maternal great-grandmother had been a slave. The student found that reading about something, then discovering how close to home it was, was sobering. She said that she felt closer to her family and was planning to visit a great aunt and the rest of the family she had never met.

Films, computers, radios, videos, television, xerox machines—to name a few—may never even have been dreamed of by your grandparents. For them and their forebears, the overwhelming factor was family, not machines. The elderly were highly respected and actively participated in family life, including taking care of children. Few books and magazines were available and minimal formal education was required for earning a living. Respect for authority was, more or less, taken for granted and individual initiative was not encouraged much. No one worried about privacy; each family member knew his place, felt secure and cared for. Most families lived in small, self-contained communities with relatives nearby. They could easily spot the model or ancestry of a physical or behavioral trait ("I took after grandpa in my build," or "Aunt Mary loved to dance, too"). Each one knew pretty much who s/he was and what was expected.

Today such self-awareness is harder to come by. Age-old patterns of living have been altered or destroyed by machines, rapid growth of cities and population and eased mobility, as well as a startling decrease in family size, along with increased demand for education and specialized skills and increase in divorce. As a consequence of these inroads on free time, most of us grow up with vague knowledge of our forebears.

Recall as best you can the past generations of your family, from your own to your grandparents. They total only seven people: self, two parents and four grandparents. Beyond are great-grandparents who lived 70 to 80 years ago and underwent many experiences like yours and may have been like you—genetics coming into play—in myriad ways. However, you may know as little about them as you do an acquaintance.

As for other relatives, many may live anywhere from several states to half the globe away. Such a condition may invariably induce a sense of discontinuity, reinforcing misunderstandings and feelings of aloneness, as expressed in the following:

> Gathering facts and material for this family history assignment proved difficult for me because I am the only one of my family living in the United States. I am indebted to my mother in Switzerland who invested a great deal of time into interviewing relatives over the phone and reminiscing. . . . Communicating by mail and phone about family brought us closer . . . having to reflect on my life also made me realize that living apart from my kin will have an impact on the upbringing of my children. Their heritage on their maternal side will not become a part of their lives. This assignment makes me re-evaluate my motivation to stay in the U.S. . . . the price for my achievements here may well be too high. B.H.

Whether you grew up in a nuclear, extended or single-parent family, those closest to you presumably profoundly shaped your life. Many of your experiences have been formally recorded in perhaps a family bible, birth certificate, school diploma, award, citation(s), legally required photos (passport, driver's license), and other identification. But such documentation mirrors only a fraction of the efforts and circumstances that brought them about. In total these not only reflect the stories behind them, but also imply cultural continuity despite change that characterized our civilization.

As you assemble, then compare information about your parents' and grandparents' life with your own, you may detect patterns of behavior common in all three. Having blue eyes, for example, or a passion for a particular food, skill, or activity. It is believed that the family preoccupation of Alexander Graham Bell with problems of speaking and hearing may have presaged his invention of the telephone. His paternal grandfather had been an actor and elocutionist and wrote a book on phonetics as a means of curing stammering. Later his father and paternal uncle made their livelihood teaching these same elocution techniques. Alexander's mother and wife were both deaf and he, himself, taught the deaf.

Such repetitive patterns of behavior through several generations illustrate that to know only the history of your life and that of your immediate family is to understand just a small part of yourself. The poet William Wordsworth may have had this in mind when he suggested that should you hold a baby to your ear, sounds of centuries will you hear. Recognition of generational patterns of behavior is dramatically featured in Sophocles' *Oedipus Rex,* Shakespeare's *Romeo and Juliet* and *King Lear,* and even in the popular soap-opera family of *Dallas.*

As a potentially rewarding and enduring hobby your family history also has an advantage: one of being the least expensive to pursue and easily picked up as desired. It may prove more cherished than a photo album—in short, an heirloom for generations to come.

The instructions and materials needed are in this book. You will direct your own research, your teacher serving as technical advisor. Once underway your enterprise may entice family members, even bring them closer, as discovered by one such researcher who wrote, "I have learned so much about my past. Talking to my mother and grandmother and her siblings really gets me more in touch with them and their lives." S.R.

This research may also evoke questions about family members otherwise taken for granted—that although you can fluently describe how you feel about them, it may surprise you to discover how superficially you know them. As one student remarked:

> I learned that my grandmother had six brothers. This came as a surprise because my mother, my uncle and my aunt only knew of three brothers. . . . one died of appendicitis at age sixteen, another while serving in the Army or Airforce during World War I and drowned in the Panama Canal. I wish my grandmother were alive so I could ask her why she had never mentioned them." M.H.

And another:

> ". . . while talking to my mother about our family history, I learned that my mother had a brother before she was born who died of rheumatic fever at age twenty-one. I was shocked because I had never heard of my deceased uncle from any family member. My mother said it was because she never knew him either, since he died before she was born . . ." R.O.

A new insight may prove disturbing as expressed here:

"Talking with one of my grandmother's nephews, I learned that my great grandparents were really not happy that my grandmother was marrying an Italian because in her day, the Irish and Italians did not get along." M.H.

A colleague mentioned to me that he regrets that he knows almost nothing about his grandparents because, as a young man, he had never realized what questions to ask his parents or how to ask them. It might well be a test of maturity to learn how to phrase the questions without embarrassment to yourself or the other person.

Perhaps our present, ultra-mobile society, coupled with rapid sociological and technological change, has increased alienation between family members and particularly between generations. The inevitable result is a rootlessness and lack of identity, such as must have afflicted orphans in the days of close family ties when children had a sense of belonging and the anchor of traditional values.

Many Czechoslovakian writers, for example, in expressing their horror about the previous Communist Czechoslovakian regime, mourned that it tried by every expedient to expunge the national memory of centuries of struggle for national independence. Sociologists have a word for the spiritual paralysis of living without social context or values: *anomie*.

Researching your family history gives you an opportunity to alleviate, to some degree, that sense of estrangement from the currents of life.

ADDITIONAL STUDENT OBSERVATIONS

"The most important thing I learned was how my father and grandfather worked so hard to get where they are. My grandfather worked two jobs, six days a week, just to eat and feed his family. My father had to work to put himself through college. It makes me feel guilty in a way that after all my father did to get where he is, my life looks like a cakewalk. It has taught me to take on more responsibility in my life." G.F.

"I found out that it was my grandmother's father who was born in Russia. Because the parents did not want their son to have to serve in the Armed Forces, they cut off his thumb of his right hand so he could not be able to shoot a gun." A.C.

"My grandmother still lives in Williamsburg, and in the same house that all her children were born in. I get the sense that she may favor her eldest son because there are lots of war pictures of him. My mother said it was because grandmother was very worried about him in the Korean War. I also saw a picture of my grandfather, (my real one), which I never saw before and found out that my grandmother wore slacks once or twice and has never worn them again.'' G.B.

"I found out that my last name went through a few changes. . . . My grandfather and Eddie Cantor, the actor, were first cousins. The name was eventually changed again to the one my great-grandmother's step-father had. . . . She chose this name because she loved him very much." A.C.

"Because I am an American-born Chinese, there is much I do not know about my Oriental background." C.L.

Chapter Two

Charting Your Direction

In planning a trip it is prudent to secure directions. It minimizes the risk of long, tedious or even dangerous detours, but more importantly, may make your journey more enjoyable and perhaps even pleasantly memorable. Much the same need applies to rewarding research in family history. The assignments may strike you at first as detours but, as noted, their aim in the long run is to facilitate your efforts and provide you with awakening challenges.

A. Assignment #1—Examine your assumptions
Suggested steps: (1) Class discussion
(2) Homework

Preliminary wisdom in research is to dissect out your assumptions, above all the tacit—unspoken, unverbalized, willy-nilly unexamined, inherited prejudices—and those that rubbed off your contemporaries. The dictionary defines an assumption as, "the act of supposing or taking for granted."

Much in life one takes for granted simply because of earlier experience and bruising collisions with realities. It has naturally led you to expect that which was so in the past will be so in the future. As a consequence, much of your behavior becomes automatic as, for example, reaching for the light switch on the left or right side of the wall when you enter a dark room, or expecting your bus to arrive on time, even your instructor. Most often, such assumptions are essential, time-saving means of freeing one's mind, the better to cope with day-to-day living. But where you have only limited experience with a subject, you're likely to harbor shaky assumptions, e.g., that fat people are apt to be jolly, that all Latins gesticulate avidly or that, in a dispute between labor and management, labor is always right. Thoughts falling into this category are denoted as prejudices.

Assumptions however—those having good statistical odds—can also be used as valuable investigative tools. Police detectives, for example, in trying to solve a crime, use an approach like: "Let's assume that the victim knew his assailant," or, "What if the victim came in unexpectedly?"

Corporations in their annual reports to shareholders strive to forecast future dividends based on their assumption on how the market is likely to perform, or their products and innovations will find favor, and that money spent in advertising will not be wasted.

Still other assumptions may be nothing more than resistance in disguise, a form of laziness too, perhaps, by telling yourself that what you already know about a subject is sufficient. That's when the "buts" crowd in. Among those I've encountered most frequently in Family History research are:

(1) But I already know a lot about my family, more, in fact, than I care to know;

(2) But my parents are divorced (or one parent is deceased), and I hardly ever see my mother/father, so I'll probably be unable to extract the information I need;

(3) But I was adopted and I don't know who my real parents are, so I can't really research my real family history;

(4) But my parents may think I'm prying if I start asking them questions about their lives that I never asked before;

(5) But my stepmother/stepfather raised me and I've had no contact whatsoever with my real parents since I was very small;

(6) But my parents weren't born in this country and all family documents, photos and other things I'll need for this research were lost during the war. I don't think I can do justice to this project.

All these and, perhaps, more assumptions include obstacles which, in reality, offer opportunities for finding direction. To explore each in turn:

(1) But I already know a lot about my family, more, in fact, than I care to know.

Humans are like icebergs in that more than 90% of their lives, i.e., experiences, memories, feelings, are buried in a sea of preoccupation. All we seem to know of them is what we see and hear in our daily interactions. Take a closer look at your parents. Chances are you see them as your guardians, disciplinarians and decision-makers and, however imperfect, as models. Because of child-parent relationship, you may not often have the intimate give-and-take as that which you enjoy with your peers. You're bound to forget at times that your mom and dad are individuals in their own right. After you've researched their lives through direct interviews and other sources, you may be likelier to find what some students who started out with that unexamined assumption found:

". . . I learned something that surprised me. For most of my life, I 'blamed' my paternal ancestors for 'burdening' me with my small stature (actually, it isn't a burden; it can even be advantageous, at times). My mother's cousin informed me that my maternal great-grandmother was also five feet nothing and full of hype and energy. I also learned that she was a compulsive cleaner. Perhaps now, I know where my need to keep everything almost spotlessly clean comes from." A.D.

"Goodness know, without this research, I may never have found out that my mother's first cousin was a midget." O.Z.

"This report helped me to know my mom better, how she behaved as a child, how her environment helped her become the person that she is today. I also enjoyed hearing about my grandmother. She died a year before I was born . . . E.R.

(2) But my parents are divorced (or one parent is deceased) and I hardly ever see my mother/father, so I'll probably be unable to extract the information I need.

Where parents are divorced, or one parent is deceased, the surviving parent, grandparents and/or siblings of the missing parent most likely can provide much of the information needed.

(3) But I was adopted and I don't know who my real parents are, so I can't research my real family history.

Your stumbling block is the word *real*. *Real* parents are those who adopted you, cared for you from your earliest years and whose influence, values, norms, etc., contributed most to the formation of your personality.

(4) But my parents may think I'm prying if I start asking them questions about their lives that I never asked before.

An actual quotation:

> "As I began to explain the project in researching my family history, my father seemed glad to help. However, when I began to ask him questions, he became defensive and his answers were very short. He did not elaborate on any personal stories." A.C.

When you soberly define the project, and that you need not include anything embarrassing or compromising, your parents are likely to cooperate. Also, it may be helpful if you showed Chapter One of this guidebook, entitled: *WHO AM I?* to your parents.

If, however, you find that one or both of your parents prove adamant (a first in my experience), then opt for the family history of a friend, or an historical figure you admire.

(5) But my stepmother/stepfather raised me, and I've had no contact whatsoever with one of my real parents ever since, so there's not much information I can get.

You still have one parent readily available from whom you can get information, including, no doubt, several close relatives, so get on with it.

(6) But my parents weren't born in this country and all family documents, photos and other things I'll need for this research were lost during the war. I don't think I can do justice to this project.

Through direct interviews with your parents, you can still get considerable information about their country and conditions that prevailed during their early years. This can be supplemented with library research. For additional clues for finding missing documents, check out the section at the end of Chapter Three entitled, "Partial Checklist of Possible Sources."

B. Assignment #2—Define your terms
Suggested steps: (1) Class discussion
(2) Library work

Words are symbols, abstract or concrete, for your thoughts. These symbols enable the human species to record the doings of past generations. The words we use most often also set borders around our thinking. Take a seemingly concrete word, "table." Unless you add the necessary specific word, e.g., "Lamp table," "cocktail table," "dining table," etc., your reader won't be clear about what you mean. It can also be abstract, as one "tables a resolution". Such is likely to happen when you use such abstract words as, "culture," "religions," "creative," "liberal," etc. One can't predict with certainty the images these words create in the listener's head.

In historical research certain much-used words are abstractions—all the more reason for insuring that the meaning you intend is as accurate and specific as possible. The purpose of this assignment, therefore, is for you to look up the definitions of the following terms, using the latest standard dictionary, as well as authoritative texts, i.e., sociological treatises, specialized books on family, kinship, etc. You may wish to add a few more words to this list:

Family	Kinship
Generation	Ethnic
History	Race
Primary source	Secondary source
Generation	Genealogy
Sibling	Culture
Culture shock	Enculturation
Ethnocentric	Era

C. Assignment #3—Review the literature:
Suggested steps: (1) Library work
(2) Class discussion

As beneficiaries and creators of culture, we must often find out what our lives are all about—what does it mean to be alive in our particular society at this particular time—and amid the buzzing confusions engendered by changes in technology, and meeting, even working with people from different backgrounds. From the handaxe of the Australopithicene to computers and scientific medicine, we have struggled to adapt to the present world. The struggle goes on. Over the centuries evidence of this struggle surfaces in journals, diaries, letters, biographies and autobiographies, as well as family histories. Most appealing, as indicated by weekly book sales, are the autobiographies and biographies which are, in part, family histories since most narrators include substantial information about their forebears.

This assignment, then, is for you to peruse 2 or 3 autobiographies, a couple of biographies, journals and diaries, not only to familiarize yourself with the diversity of personal histories that exist but, for the present purpose, to discuss these in class for comparing the various aspects of their respective histories that these authors chose to focus upon. In the course of the discussion, jot these observations and comparisons in your loose-leaf notebook for future reference. A partial list of suggested references appears at the end of this chapter.

Excerpts from the notebooks of former students may be of interest.

". . . Looking over published biographies, autobiographies, diaries and journals helped me realize that there are many different styles. Many writers concentrated on inner thoughts and emotions. The most interesting told their story in the first person, and combined personal experiences and feelings about what was happening in their families at different times." L.Z.

". . . Some authors chose to begin by stating the purpose for writing their personal history. Harry Truman, for example, explained that his autobiography was to show how a country boy grew up to become a U.S.A. president. Other authors began with a childhood story. I guess the explanation of purpose makes the work more interesting." E.I.

". . . The readings gave me an idea of how to go about putting the information together and having it sound coherent." R.T.

". . . Reading histories, biographies and autobiographies taught me that there are many ways of writing family history. I don't know yet which style I'm going to use, but at least now I have more options." M.W.

". . . When you gave the assignment to examine various types of approaches to Family History, fear of writing my own started to diminish. Seeing what others have done gave me some ideas that I plan to follow." A.C.

". . . Like the books I've read for this assignment, I, too, intend to show how the era in which one lives affects one's life, and how society has altered lifestyles through time." J.N.

". . . I learned of various family backgrounds, customs, and lineages. Also, the readings helped me figure out an easier approach to my own future write-up and expanded my knowledge of the field. The assignment also helped me learn how to better use the library facilities." J.S.

". . . These books are not just historical data. They provide insights into the main character. I want my work to be like that, . . . to be enlightening, . . . to understand why I believe in the things I do." M.N.

Suggested Readings

Abbott, Edward C. *We Pointed Them North: Recollections of a Cowpuncher* put into writing by Helena H. Smith (New York: Farrar, Straus & Giroux, Inc., 1939)

Adams, Henry *The Education of Henry Adams: An Autobiography* (Boston: Houghton Mifflin Co., 1918)

Augustine *Confessions* Translated by Julie Kerman (New York: Doubleday & Co., 1962)

Baker, Russell *Growing Up* (New York: St. Martin's Press, 1982)

Darwin, Charles *The Autobiography of Charles Darwin* (New York: Harcourt Brace Jovanovich, Inc., 1958)

Fergusson, Harvey *Home In the West: An Inquiry Into My Origins* (New York: Duell, Sloan & Pearce, 1944)

Gallagher, Dorothy *Hannah's Daughters: Six Generations of An American Family* 1876–1976 (New York: Crowell, 1976)

Gibbon, Edward *Memoirs of My Life* (New York: Funk & Wagnall's Co., 1969)

Glasgow, Ellen *The Women Within* (New York: Harcourt Brace & Jovanovich, Inc., 1954)

Goertzel, V. & Goertzel, M.G. *Cradles of Eminence* (Boston: Little, Brown & Co., 1962)

Goldberg, Michel *Name Sake* (New Haven: Yale University Press, 1980 & 1982)

Haley, Alex *The Saga of An American Family* (New York: Doubleday & Co., 1976)

James, Henry *A Small Boy and Others* (New York: Charles Scribner's Sons, 1913)

————. *Notes of a Son and Brother* (New York: Charles Scribner's Sons, 1914)

Jones, Rufus M. *A Small Town Boy* (New York: MacMillan, 1941)

Keller, Helen *The Story of My Life,* with Her Letters: 1887–1901 (New York: Doubleday & Co., 1947)

Lewisohn, Ludwig *Up Stream: An American Chronicle* (New York: Random House, 1926)

Lipton, Betty Jean *Memoirs Of An Adopted Daughter: Twice Born* (New York: Penguin, 1976)

Misch, George *A History of Autobiography In Antiquity* (Cambridge, MA: Harvard University Press, 1951)

McKuen, Rod *Finding My Father: One Man's Search For Identity* (New York: Coward-McCann, 1976)

Panunzio, Constantine M. *The Soul Of An Immigrant* (New York: Macmillan, 1921)

Standin, Nika *Reminiscence & Ravioli* (New York: William Morrow & Co., 1946)

Ullman, Liv *Changing* (New York: Alfred A. Knopf, 1977)

Washington, Booker T. *Up From Slavery: An Autobiography* (Boston: Houghton Mifflin, 1928)

Wright, Richard *Black Boy: A Record of Childhood and Youth* (New York: The World Publishing Co., 1945)

Wharton, Edith *A Backward Glance* (New York: Appleton-Century-Crofts imprint of P-H, 1934)

Yogananda, Paramahansa *The Autobiography Of A Yoga* (Los Angeles: Self Realization Fellowship, 1959)

References

Baldwin, Christina *One To One: Self Understanding Through Journal Writing* (New York: M. Evans & Co., 1977)

Bradshaw, John *The Family: A Revolutionary Way of Self Discovery* (Deerfield Beach, FL: Health Communications, 1988)

Carruth, G. *The Encyclopedia of American Facts & Dates* (8th Edition), (New York: Harper & Row, 1987)

Case, Patricia Ann *How To Write Your Autobiography,* or *Preserving Your Family Heritage* (Santa Barbara, CA: Woodbridge Press Publishing Co., 1977)

Dragnin, Yaffa *The Family Historians Handbook* (New York: Harcourt Brace Jovanovich, 1978)

Gordon, A. & Lois *Six Decades In American Life: 1920–1980* (New York: Atheneum, 1987)

Heslop, J.M. & von Orden, D. *How To Write Your Personal History* (Salt Lake City, UT: Bookcraft Inc., 1976)

———. *How To Find Anyone, Anywhere* (Eden Press: 11623 Slater "E", P.O. Box 8410, Fountain Valley, CA 92728)

Quarterly Journal of The American Name Society

Quarterly Stepfamily Bulletin (Stepfamily Association of America, Inc., 213 Centennial Mall, S., Suite 212, Lincoln, NE 68508)

Phillimore, P.W. *How To Write The History of A Family* (Owings Hall, MD: Sternmer House Publishing, Inc., 1983)

Stetson, Oscar F. *The Art of Ancestor Hunting: A Guide to Ancestral Research and Genealogy* (New York: Daye Press, 1965, 1946, 1936)

Toman, W. *Family Constellation: Its Effect on Personality and Social Behavior* (New York: Springer Publishing Co., 1976)

Visher, John *Stepfamilies: Myths and Realities* (Secaucus, NJ: Citadel Press, 1979)

Weinstein, R.A. & Booth, L. *The Collection, Use & Care of Historical Photographs* (Nashville: American Association For State & Local History, 1976)

Weitzman, David *Underfoot: The Everyday Guide to Exploring America's Past* (New York: Charles Scribner's Sons, 1976)

Chapter Three

Specifics—Getting Started

As indicated, you will be your own researcher in exploring perhaps new territory, and also perhaps arriving at a new understanding of family with your teacher serving as technical guide. There are three sorts of operations: (1) Homework, (2) Class discussion and (3) Library work. This book sketches a framework for each; they overlap at times but each is designed to speed your efforts.

A. Homework:

Do study the lists of materials, sources, hints on collecting data and setting up interviews in person, (via phone, through correspondence); the instructions on how to record, select and transfer data from your looseleaf notebook onto the detailed guide sheets, the information called for under each heading, etc. Also each specific assignment you will be asked to complete will include suggestions on how best to start, e.g., homework, class discussion, and/or library work, but not necessarily in that order.

B. Class discussion:

The aim here is to promote flexibility in thinking, provide opportunities for asking questions, help check your direction, perhaps, freshen motivation and enliven an atmosphere of useful give-and-take.

C. Library work:

To further familiarize yourself with the many styles a family history may take, continue to examine personal journals, biographies and autobiographies. The experience may stimulate recall of anecdotes told you by family members.

Also, to learn about historical events and transformation during each of the three generations, you will almost surely need to examine background historical texts in your college or local town library.

After you've completed an assignment, file it in the appropriate folder, i.e., Self, Mother/Father or Maternal grandmother/Paternal grandfather. When ready to set down the first draft of your family history, reread each completed assignment for whatever anecdotes or other information you judge important for inclusion—or perhaps emphasis in the final draft. Here's an example from Assignment #2, in Chapter Two, excerpted by a former student:

". . . As the author, Michael Goldberg did in his autobiography, *Name Sake,* I, too, would like to analyze events in the past so as to build up my family history. By including episodes from my looseleaf, I expect to show how I'm being affected by the present historical and political forces." M.H.

Your written description derived from the assignment on how you see yourself, your parent and grandparent may well contribute to your final draft. The same could be said for all the other completed assignments, as well.

D. Some Guidelines:

(1) WHERE TO START:

At home!
Everyone who is relevant and within reach and everything to the purpose—old photos, old letters received, ledgers, family records, badges, certificates, diplomas, military discharge papers, and other official documents including old bank books, deeds, receipts, etc. (See the chart at the end of this chapter for additional lists of research sources.)

(2) SOME MATERIALS YOU WILL NEED:

- A loose-leaf notebook (comfortable pocket size)
- Several ball-point pens
- Several #2 pencils (Librarians allow researchers to work *only* in pencil)

• Manila folders (one for each person marked as follows: *Self; Mother/Father; Maternal Grandmother/Paternal Grandfather; Comparative Analysis of Data; Miscellaneous*)
• A large cardboard box (to house photos, folders, mementos, documents, correspondence, photocopies and all other relevant materials)
• Paste for mounting copies of photos and/or documents (to prevent original photos and documents from deteriorating, use only acid-free paper and *no* glue)
• Typing paper for writing up final draft
• Book folder or binder for final draft

(3) OPTIONAL MATERIALS:

• A tape recorder and six two-hour blank tapes*
• Six postcards
• Letter writing paper
• Number 10 business envelopes
• Postage stamps
• Brodart, Inc. 1609 Memorial Avenue, Williamsport, PA 17701 (for their colored catalogue of supplies of equipment used by libraries for organizing and preserving records.)

(4) SOME RESEARCH TIPS:

• To avoid risk of smearing information sources, use pencil only
• Use only one side of the paper in your looseleaf and all other drafts
• Strive for complete accuracy in copying information of dates, proper names as recorded on documents, including place names, map captions, dates printed, etc.
• Copy full name as legally recorded. Put nicknames in parenthesis, e.g., Mabel Laura Jones (Bella).
• Always indicate in footnotes where, how and when you got your information and from whom
• Where the exact date of an event is in question, use the words "about", "circa" or "ca."
• Record exactly as printed in this order: city, county, state.
• If marriage date is unknown but husband's birthdate is, add 25 years from his birthdate for husband and 21 for wife.

---

*Although recorded interviews of family members may become valuable keepsakes, they may later have to be transcribed for ready reference in writing your final draft.

- Record exactly as printed in this order: month, day, year.
- List children's names in order of birth. Approximate the unknown date of birth(s) as two years apart.
- Use these common abbreviations for denoting kinship:

M	= male	F	= female
gr	= great	neph	= nephew
gd	= grand	rem	= removed

- Make two copies of final draft (one for your instructor). Do not include original photos, documents, letters and mementos with the copy submitted. Do include, however, a signed and dated copy of the permission letter to your instructor, a sample of which appears on pg. 21
- Mount and label every photo, news clipping and/or document pertaining to each subject. Enclose in a separate, large envelope and place in his/her file.
- If a date is illegible, estimate and footnote this fact on the detailed guidesheet(s) where relevant

(5) SUGGESTIONS FOR RESEARCH CORRESPONDENCE

- Keep copies of all letters you send out and replies you may receive.
- Be brief, concise; limit your request to one or two details only, making sure to enclose a stamped, self-addressed envelope
- Always ask in your letter for the record, volume and page from which the information you requested was acquired.
- Be sure your letter is easy to read; whenever possible, type it or write legibly with a ballpoint pen. Include your address on the letter itself, as well as on the envelope.
- When requesting duplicate copies of records, be sure to ask what, if any, fee is involved.
- When writing to public offices, town clerks, etc., a stamped, self-addressed envelope is unnecessary.
- Offer to pay for photostat copies.
- Confine your letter to one simple request and ask about only *one* person or subject at a time.

SAMPLE RESEARCH PROJECT RELEASE

_____
Date

TO:

   FOR VALUABLE CONSIDERATION, I agree to participate in the
FAMILY HISTORY RESEARCH PROJECT being conducted by
Professor Valentine Rossilli Winsey, and hereby irrevocably consent
to and authorize the use and reproduction by Prof. Winsey and/or
Pace University ("Pace"), or anyone authorized by Prof. Winsey or
Pace, of any and all written materials that I have submitted or may
submit while enrolled in any of Prof. Winsey's courses or otherwise,
including but not limited to all class assignments and reports, and all
written or oral responses that I have given or may give in connection
with said project, and any photographs, tape recordings or video
tapes of interviews that I have given or may give, by Prof. Winsey,
and Pace's employees, agents, representatives or designees, for any
purposes whatsoever, without further compensation to me. The
written materials that I have submitted or may submit and the written
or oral responses which I have given or may give and photographs,
tape recordings and video tapes of said interviews, shall constitute the
sole property of Prof. Winsey and Pace University. I further authorize
the use and reproduction by Prof. Winsey and/or Pace of my
comments, in any manner and on the same terms as set forth above.

                              _____
                              Student

                              _____
                              (Parent or Guardian if
                              Student under 18 years)

WITNESS:

_____

PARTIAL CHECK LIST OF POSSIBLE SOURCES

What To Look For	Where To Look For It	Where To Write Away For It*

I. RECORD OF BIRTH

Birth Certificate	Family Bible,	Board of Health
Baptismal Certificate	especially inside	(Local Office)
Bris	flyleaf	Hospital where event
Bar (Bat) mitzva	Surviving	occurred
Communion	pediatrician, and/or	Local church where
Certificate	midwife	subject lived at the
Confirmation	Local or town	time
Certificates	photographer	Local temple where
Geographic Loc.	Consult Civil Records	subject lived at the
climate	& Church Records	time
environmental	Books—family photo	Bureau of Vital
features	album, ask parents,	Statistics in town of
Mass Cards	ask relatives, god	birth
Family Letters &	parents, Reference	U.S. Census Bureau
announcements	Librarian, Special	which not only tells
	Libraries—	a person's
	genealogical ones	birthplace, but his
	for ship passenger	trade, as well
	lists	Superintendent of
	World Atlas	Documents
		U.S. Gov't Printing Office
		Washington, D.C. 20402
		Adoptee's Liberation Movement, a self-help group geared to finding records of birth & adoption which include names and identities of principles involved

---

*For those who have immigrant forebears, write to: U.S. Immigration and Naturalization Service Office, 421 I Street, N.W., Washington, D.C. 20536

PARTIAL LIST OF RESEARCH SOURCES (cont'd)

What To Look For	Where To Look For It	Where To Write Away For It
II. NUMBER OF SIBLINGS		
Same as above, plus	Family Bible	Funeral parlor
Insurance policies	Family Records—	Cemetary plot deeds
Death Certificates	files, bank vault,	Attending
	relatives, parents	physician(s)
		Bureau of Vital
		Statistics
III. SCHOOL		
Transcripts	Grammar School	Private or Public
Diplomas	Album	Grammar/High/
Awards	High School—	Junior High
Licenses	Awards,	The school Principal
Certificates	Certificates	The Board of
Other	Graduation Diplomas	Education in the
	Trade &/or	town in which
	Professional	subject resided in
	Organizations	childhood
	School Yearbooks of	College &/or
	various kinds	University
	Scrapbooks	Registrar's Office
	Letters, postcards	Trade or Professional
	(old ones)	Organization which
		issued the license/
		Certificate

PARTIAL LIST OF RESEARCH SOURCES (cont'd)

What To Look For	Where To Look For It	Where To Write Away For It

IV. *RECORD OF PAID EMPLOYMENT*

What To Look For	Where To Look For It	Where To Write Away For It

Age at first paid employment
Place-type work—no. hrs., wkly wages, working conditions
Business
  Tax Records
  Contract(s)
  Deed(s)
  Mortgage
  Retirement Pension
  Records
Social Security
Stocks/Bonds/Check books/Appointment books/Calendars/
Savings Account books/Safe Deposit box/Wills
	See listing to left under Business IV friends, co-workers, relatives photos, correspondence
	Family file boxes or drawers
		Social Security Office

PARTIAL LIST OF RESEARCH SOURCES (cont'd)

What To Look For	Where To Look For It	Where To Write Away For It
V. LEISURE TIME ACTIVITIES		

Hobbies	Diaries
	Old Cookbooks
	Photo Albums
	Safety Deposit Box
	  books, coins,
	  stamps, postcards,
	  heirlooms, theatre
	  programs, old
	  family recipes,
	  other, etc.
		Old friends, perhaps
		  colleagues,
		  business associates

Vacation & Travel Activities
Passports
Souvenirs
Postcards
Photo Albums
Immigration
  (Naturalizaton
  Papers)
	Family files
	Old Correspondence
		See above

VI. MARRIAGE		

Printed
  announcement/
  invitation
Marriage license
Newspaper notices
Anniversary
  mementos
Divorce decrees
Re-marriages
Other
	See Listing for
	  Section I	

PARTIAL LIST OF RESEARCH SOURCES (cont'd)

What To Look For	*Where To Look For It*	*Where To Write Away For It*
VII. *MILITARY EXPERIENCE*		
Service induction papers, etc., promotion/ citations; discharge papers, other		Military service records, *National Archives & Records Service* Washington, D.C. 20408
Pension Records		
Record of gov't land bounty given to honorably discharged soldier as reward for war service		State Adjutant General (get address from local library); contact state library in Albany Empire Plaza Albany, N.Y. 12234
VIII. *AFFILIATIONS*		
Religious Political Immigration dates: departure arrival Citizenship Ethnic nationality; racial affiliations		U.S. Immigration & Naturalization Service (Office 425 I Street, N.W. Washington, D.C. 20536

PARTIAL LIST OF RESEARCH SOURCES (cont'd)

What To Look For	Where To Look For It	Where To Write Away For It

IX. GENERATIONAL MATERIAL

What To Look For	Where To Look For It	Where To Write Away For It
Great Depression of the 30's	Local Library	
Agricultural Age	Periodicals	
Victorian "Gilded Age" in USA	Encyclopedias	
Industrial Revolution	Home files	
Atomic Age	memorabilia	
Wars/Inventions/ Discoveries	photographs	
U.S. Presidents, etc.	souvenirs	
Famous Personalities	postcards	
songs	letters	
musicals	old theatre playbills	
comedies & operas	Historical Sources	
painters	books	
writers	articles, etc.	
	Historical Societies	
	are likely to have	
	vertical files	
	containing copies of	
	deeds, wills,	
	articles on	
	neighborhood	
	'happenings'	

PARTIAL LIST OF RESEARCH SOURCES (cont'd)

What To Look For	*Where To Look For It*	*Where To Write Away For It*
X. *HEALTH PROFILE*		
vaccination certificate	Death Certificates for	Relatives
medical, drug	causes listed	Friends
prescriptions	hospital bills, Get	Family doctor
gift cards/	well cards	
correspondence	Gravestones	
insurance		
HIP/HMO		
Blue Cross/		
Blue Shield		
other		
Death certificate		
notices (newspaper		
obituary (ies and		
eulogies)		
wills		
Medicare, Medicaid		
documents		

XI. *Family anecdotes, proverbs, legends, stories, etc.*
(These are usually passed down by word-of-mouth)

STILL MORE POSSIBLE SOURCES (cont'd)

- Note names and dates on *all* sources
- Family Records
- Outside Sources

Some associations or societies may require a fee for their services. (A self-addressed, stamped envelope generally insures a reply.) When requesting copies of documents, be sure to state names and dates.

—Bureau of Vital Statistics
  125 Worth Street
  New York, N.Y. 10013

—U.S. Immigration and Naturalization Service Offices
  425 I Street, Northwest
  Washington D.C. 20536

—Application of Search of Census Records
BC 600 Personal Census Service Branch
Bureau of the Census
Pittsburgh, KS 66732

—Military Service Records
NNCC/GSA
National Archives and Records Service
Washington D.C. 20408

—Guide to Genealogical Records
National Archives
Washington D.C. 20408

—National Archives
Washington D.C. 20408
(Central U.S. depository for records in Washington local branch is in
Bayonne, NJ)

N.B.   Most local libraries have the U.S. Census on microfilm

—New York Public Library
Local History & Genealogy Room
Fifth Avenue & 42nd Street
New York, N.Y. 10018
(Houses the largest collection of maps and atlases in the country.) Also 20
volumes that comprise the *Dictionary Catalog of Local History and
Genealogy* by G.K. Hall

—Church of Jesus Christ of Latterday Saints "Mormons"
50 East North Temple Street
Salt Lake City, Utah 84150
(Has the largest repository of family genealogical information in the world.
Write for information on branch nearest you.)

—Mormon Genealogy Center

—New Jersey Historical Society
230 Broadway
Newark, N.J.

—Ye Old Genealogie Shoppe
9430 Vandegriff Road
Indianapolis, Indiana

—New York Genealogical and Biographical Society
122 East 58th Street
New York, N.Y. 10022

—American Genealogist
1232 39th Street
Des Moines, Iowa 50311

—National Genealogical Society Quarterly
1921 Sunderland Place, N.W.
Washington D.C. 20036

—Genealogical Helper
Everton Publishers
P.O. Box 368
Logan, Utah 84321

*
Some Possible Obstacles

—Boundaries may have changed over the years re. international, national, state or local levels.
—Ancestor's names may have also been changed—note spelling.
—Scarce records before 20th century may make it difficult to research Blacks and women.
—Be skeptical of genealogical professionals, so-called, who solicit your interest (and money!)

*
Still Other Sources

—*Webster's New International Dictionary of the English Language,* Second Edition, unabridged G&C Mirriam Co., Springfield, MA, '55.
—*Webster's Geographical Dictionary*
—*Lippincott's Pronouncing Gazeteer,* Revised Edition, Edited by J. Thomas, M.S. and Baldwin, Phil., J.B. Lippincott & Co., 1972
—*Historical Gazeteer* Lewis' Topographical Dictionaries of the British Isles lists locations for England, Wales, Scotland and Ireland.
—*Ballinger's Postal Guide*—lists post offices only, but may help in identifying certain towns.
—*Maps*—for communities, valleys, historical areas, church parishes, etc.
—*Historical Maps*—also called Romance Maps such as a series in the Book of American History by James Trislow Adams, 1943 (ATLAS)
—*Historical Societies* often have old settlement maps made prior to the time the county system came into effect.

ADDENDUM:

* Also, most southern local historical societies and libraries have slave auction records; second or family names of slaves, however are most often ignored.

* Quaker libraries may help with records of manumission (indicating when the slaves were freed)

Suggested Books

Consumer Guide *Tracing Your Roots* (New York: Bell Publishing Co., 1977)

Doane, Gilbert H. and James B. Bell *Searching For Your Ancestors: The How and Why of Genealogy* (5th Edition), (New York: Bantam Books, 1980)

Everton, George B. *The Handy Book For Genealogists* Originally compiled and published by Walter M. Everton (Logan, UT: Everton Publishers, 1971)

Genealogical Research (Washington, D.C.: American Society of Genealogists, 1980)

Greenwood, Val D. *The Researcher's Guide to American Genealogy* (Baltimore, MD: Genealogical Pub., 1974, 1973)

Kyvig, David E. and Myron A. Marty *Your Family History: A Handbook for Research Writing* (Arlington Heights, IL: AHM Publishing Corp., 1978)

McKuen, Rod *Finding My Father: One Man's Search For Identity* (New York: Coward-McCann, 1976)

Phillimore, P.W. *How To Write The History of A Family: A Guide for the Genealogist* (2nd Edition), (London: E. Stock, 1888)

Pine, L.G. (Leslie Gilbert) *American Origins* (Baltimore, MD: Genealogical Pub. Co., 1967, 1960)

Pine, L.G. (Leslie Gilbert) *The Genealogist's Encyclopedia* (New York: Weybright & Talley, 1969)

Rottenberg, Dan *Finding Our Fathers: A Guidebook to Jewish Genealogy* (1st Edition), (New York: Random House, 1977)

Visher, Emily B. *Stepfamilies: A Guide to Working with Stepparents and Stepchildren* (Secaucus, NJ: Citadel Press, 1979)

Visher, John S. and Emily B. *Stepfamilies: Myths and Realities* (Secaucus, NJ: Citadel Press, subsidiary of Carol Publishing Group, 1980)

Walker, James D. *Black Genealogy: How to Begin* (Athens, GA: University of Georgia, Center for Continuing Education, 1977)

Weitzman, David *Underfoot: An Everyday Guide to Exploring The American Past* (New York: Charles Scribner's Sons, 1976)

Westin, Jeane Eddy *Finding Your Roots: How Every American Can Trace His Ancestors at Home and Abroad* (New York: Ballatine Books, 1977)

Williams, Ethel W. *Know Your Ancestors: A Guide to Genealogical Research* (Rutland, VT: C.E. Tuttle Co., 1972, 1960)

Some Books on Surnames

Hook, J.N. (Julius Nicholas) *Family Names: The Origins, Meanings, Mutations, and History of More Than 2,800 American Names* (1st Collier Books Edition), (New York: Collier Books; London: Collier Macmillan, 1983)

Puckett, Newbell Niles *Black Names in America: Origins and Usage* Collected by Newbell Niles Puckett; Edited by Murray Heller (Boston: G.K. Hall, 1975)

Smith, Elsdon Coles *American Surnames* (Baltimore, MD: Genealogical Pub. Co., 1986, 1969)

Chapter Four
Time: Personal and Historical

Don't waste life in doubts and fears; spend yourself on the work before you, well assured that the right performance of this hour's duties will be the best preparation for the hours of ages to follow it.

Emerson

Humans may be the only creatures aware of time as such. We experience it through periodically recurrent changes, e.g., hunger pangs, sleep and wakefulness, day and night and such progressive, irreversible, biological changes from birth to maturity to death. Erik Erikson maintained that one's very identity is built on the dimension of time (Erikson, 1968).

You begin early on to pinpoint in time such milestones as first day of school, first crush, achievement award, wage-earning job, promotion, etc. You're likely to think back on these while looking ahead with perhaps growing awareness of just how much time is needed for meeting social, educational and economic obligations, and how much may remain unencumbered. You may also learn that one's use of time depends greatly not only upon *where* one is born, e.g., which culture, part of the world, type of government, socio-economic level, but *when,* e.g., in which historical era.

In the three eras set forth in the following chart for example, there are sharp differences between primitive (Prehistoric) man and agricultural man, and between agricultural and industrial man with respect to lifespan, number of years essential for work, learning (informal and

33

formal), eating, sleeping, personal hygiene, and optionally invested time. These, in large part, reflect changes in science-technology.

Dependent initially upon the sun for light, prehistoric humans must have spent about a third of their lifespan hunting-gathering food and about half of it sleeping. Once having learned to tame fire and make stone tools, they minimally mastered their environment. With the coming of agriculture (about 10,000 years ago), humans were on their way to communal living, leading over the centuries to towns, trade, specialized skills and tools, improved health care and an unprecedented rise in population. Their lifespan doubled. But most land-bound people in the Old World with its two-class system—nobles and peasants—had uncertain or little margin in making ends meet. Heavy taxation, unwise forestation to enlarge cultivable acreage in the face of an ever-increasing population intensified a need for change. Millions pulled up stakes and traveled to new and foreign lands in search of better opportunities.[1] Consider some excerpts from interviews with Southern European farmers who emigrated to the United States in 1910.[2]

> "I didn't know that my grandfather was a barber's apprentice when only eleven-years-old. In his time, he had to work a ten-hour day for little over a dollar, and for six days a week, too." A.M.
>
> "My father worked in the sulfur mines. When I was ten, I went with him. Things were so bad, I had to. I slept in my home every fifteen days a month, that's all. To school, I went for only two years. I went when I was six, and I went when I was seven. That's all!" F.R.

With the advent of industrialization a few hundred years ago, the scheduling of time changed radically. Thanks to advances in science, sanitation, nutrition and public health, the lifespan rose from a total of 35–45 years to 65–75. Alongside this was dramatic reduction in years devoted to wage-earning work. Whereas agricultural man was obliged to devote one-third of his life to earning his bread (or equivalent), industrial man could achieve it in one-tenth the time, enabling increase of several decades largely devoted to formal education and leisure activities.[3]

---

[1]Handlin, Oscar *The Uprooted* Boston, Little, Brown 1973.

[2]Winsey, Valentine R. A Study of The Effects of Transplantation Upon Attitudes Toward the United States of Southern Italians in New York City As Revealed By Survivors of The Mass-Migration 1887–1915 (New York University unpublished Ph.D. dissertation, 1966)

[3]Hunnucutt, B.K. *Work Without End* (Philadelphia. Temple University Press, 1989)

TOTAL TIME SPENT IN VARIOUS ACTIVITIES BY
PRIMITIVE, AGRICULTURAL & INDUSTRIAL MAN

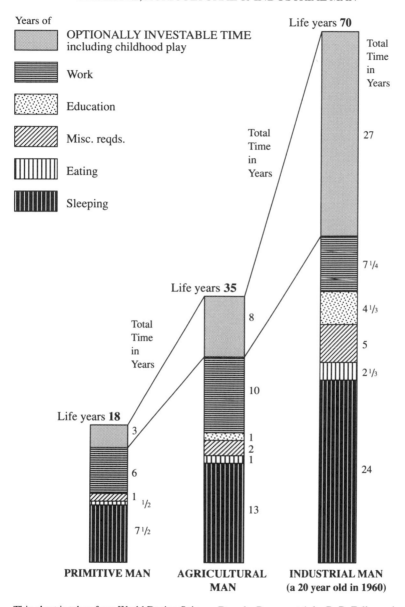

Years of

OPTIONALLY INVESTABLE TIME
including childhood play

Work

Education

Misc. reqds.

Eating

Sleeping

Life years **70**

Total
Time
in
Years

Total
Time
in
Years

27

7 1/4

4 1/3

5

2 1/3

Life years **35**

8

10

1
2
1

13

24

Total
Time
in
Years

Life years **18**

3

6

1 1/2

7 1/2

Computed from total hours spent.

PRIMITIVE MAN   **AGRICULTURAL**   **INDUSTRIAL MAN**
                          MAN   **(a 20 year old in 1960)**

This chart is taken from World Design Science Decade, Document 1, by R. B. Fuller and
J. McHale, p. 16 (S. Illinois University, 1963).

This unprecedented increase in the productive use of time by a large segment of the population is one of the incentives that spurs industrialization and encourages democracy. To maintain a fascist state, one device is to leave as little freely disposable time to the individual as possible, the rest being effectively organized by an authoritarian oligarchy. A most life-enhancing characteristic of a democracy is the time allowed to make mistakes as options are explored. This has led to deeper appreciation of free time as a resource. A review of the era of your grandparents will document a quickening decline in weekly work hours, with corresponding increase in hours for formal education and leisure. Early 20th century saw a reduction—from about 60 hours a week (1900), to 50 (1920). With the economic depression of the 1930s, a prevailing community feeling surfaced. Job-sharing and pursuit of personal interests, e.g., gardening often shared with neighbors because of enforced leisure time, decreased total weekly wage-earning hours to 35. Soon after, however, the New Deal settled on a weekly standard of 40 hours, where it has remained for the last half century, and—if spottily—decreased further with increased productivity.

"It is by the meaning that it intuitively attaches to *time* that one culture is differentiated from another," said Oswald Spengler.[4] In relatively homogeneous and isolated societies, *time* is expressed simply as an association of two natural or social events. The Nuer of Central Africa, for example, are likely to promise, "I shall return at milking," or "I shall start off when the cows come home."[5]

Many so-called "undeveloped" (non-industrialized) cultures cherish traditional somewhat casual attitudes toward *time*. If you plan a dinner party for 8:00 p.m. in Northwestern Africa be not surprised should several guests not arrive till 9 or 9:30 p.m., depending upon their social status, e.g., higher their status, later the arrival; likewise for business appointments. As E.T. Hall observes in his study, *The Silent Language*,[6] each culture uses time and space in its own way. A business appointment for 2:00 p.m. in most South American countries is interpreted as meaning that the meeting will more likely take place even as late as 3:30 p.m.

---

[4]Spengler, Oswald, 1880–1936 *The Decline of The West* (New York, Modern Library 1962, 1965)

[5]Evans-Pritchard, E.E. (Edward Evan). *The Nuer, A Description of The Modes of Livelihood and Political Institutions of the Nilotic People.* Oxford: At The Clarendon Press, 1940

[6]Hall, Edward Twitchell. *The Silent Language.* Garden City, N.Y.: Anchor Press/ Doubleday, 1973, 1959

This challenge confronted a friend when he was invited several years ago to a huge Latin American country to help organize a desperately needed, national-scale research program. The prestige of my friend—an eminent scientist—was not at issue: it was internationally recognized. Soon after arrival, he instituted a coffee session every afternoon at precisely 4:00 p.m., to last somewhere between 15 and 30 minutes, depending on whether there were visitors anxious to disclose their research plans. Formal appointments were unnecessary, it being understood that coffee began just about at 4 and would last about one half hour, and under no circumstances would there be private time for visitors however distinguished academically. For many visitors, this was a shocking introduction of the recognition of *time* as an irreplaceable resource—a recognition essential for effective tackling of the dreadful health problems faced by that country which had badly faltered, after a brilliant but unsustained beginning.

Today, more and more peasant villagers and nomadic tribes are being integrated into developing nation states. Their sense of relatively unchanging time is being radically altered by modern technology, factories, schools and the mass media. We North Americans are perhaps more conscious of time than any other culture. Wrist watches, once considered an affectation by an effete, self-styled aristocracy, for example, are the most common gift items. For a child, being given an adult-style wrist-watch, is a rite of passage. Look at your wrist. Chances are it carries a state-of-the-art, *functional* watch. You learn early indeed to depend on advanced engineering to help make the most of time. Our appreciation and preoccupation with time has been expressed in many ways. A few samples:

"We all of us complain of the shortness of time and yet have much more than we know what to do with. We are always complaining that our days are few and acting as though there would be no end of them." (Seneca 80 A.D.)

"Be not as one who has ten-thousand years to live." Marcus Aurelius

"Dost thou love life? Then waste not time, for that is the stuff life is made of." Benjamin Franklin

"The real secret of how to use time is to pack it as you would a portmanteau, filling up the small places with small things." Sir H. Haddow

"Until Youth begins to plan, the sense of self is not complete." G. Allport

"Lost, yesterday, somewhere between sunrise and sunset, two golden hours, each set with sixty diamond minutes. No reward is offered, for they are gone forever." H. Mann

"Time that is past thou never canst recall; of time to come thou are not sure at all; the present only is within thy power, so therefore now improve thy present hour." Lord Byron

A recent Random House *College Dictionary* lists about 40 different terms and phrases for *time*. Among them: *timing, ahead of time, nick of time, behind the times, old-timer, time-belt, time-lag, time-out, timeless, time-machine, bide-your-time, time and time again, in the nick of time, time and tide wait for no man, in due time, time of your life, time is up,* etc. "The reason I beat the Austrians," Napoleon said, "is that they did not know the value of five minutes." Among other things, the Duke of Wellington knew this better as demonstrated at the Battle of Waterloo which, in a matter of seconds, accomplished Napoleon's downfall.

Poets, writers, philosophers throughout the ages have speculated about time as experience. "Quoth the raven, 'Nevermore,' " wrote Poe. "The years like great black oxen tread the world," (Yeats). "Tomorrow and tomorrow and tomorrow/Creeps in this petty pace from day to day," (Shakespeare). "Truditur dies die," (One day makes way for another—Horace). "Time rolls in his ceaseless course," (Scott).

Historians have marked off progress in terms of tools and strategies of adaptation, e.g., Stone Age, Bronze Age, Iron Age, Agricultural Era, Industrial Era, Nuclear Age, Space Age—and in terms of behavior: Dark Ages, Middle Ages, Golden Age, Christian Era, Gay Nineties, Prohibition Era, Jazz Age, Depression Era, etc.

Many physicists are very much concerned with understanding *time*. They speak of *Time's arrow* and speculate endlessly as to why it is seemingly irreversible. Those among you addicted to science-fiction know that a gimmick for reversing *time* is a staple. The most famous example is a story by H.G. Wells, *The Time Machine.* For many years there was even a popular comic strip called "Alleyoop", in which the hero was a burly caveman carrying a club who, thanks to his friendship with a professor, would sometimes find himself plunged into one or another later historical period.

That *time is money* might, perhaps, well serve as one slogan of American culture. So, to summarize, a good test of democracy is how *time* becomes available to develop personal interests, ranging from nature study to learning, among other things, methods of research in undertaking family history. This was said poignantly by John Adams, president of the U.S. in a letter to his wife, Abigail, May 12th, 1780:

"I must study politics and war that my sons may have the liberty to study mathematics and philosophy."

A. Assignment #4: Your Use of Time:
Suggested steps: (1) Homework
(2) Class discussion

Your first assignment obliged you to dissect out your assumptions about delving into your family history. Consider for a moment, then, your assumptions about *time,* and how they may have changed through the years. As a child, next week's promised trip to the circus assuredly seemed an eternity away. Today you're likely to plan a vacation months ahead and think nothing of it.

How you may spend your time, i.e., ritual, leisure, work, etc., is influenced not only by your inherited socio-economic class, but also, in large part, by the era into which you were born. As a child, spending hours watching T.V. is an option unheard of by your grandparents in their childhood. Similarly, spending four years in high school or college was for them an improbable goal. For your grandparents, a wage-earning job right out of grammar school was a vital necessity.

Your assignment for the next week is to keep a daily record of how you use the hours from awakening until bedtime. Among the daily activities, please include sleep, dressing, meals, travel to and from work, school, studying and socializing and, of course, activities (no need to specify!) that you remain in good standing as a mammal (male or female).

This assignment aims to sharpen your awareness of *time* in a personal family historical context. Following are some student excerpts from the assignment about *Time:*

"I always try to divide my time for this and that. For example, 1 hour for studying History, 2 hours for Accounting, 1 hour for T.V. watching, 1 hour for eating, etc. Although I always end up spending more time on one thing than I had planned, I still try to follow through as much as possible. The portrait I got of me is of a person who is always trying to be organized, trying to do everything the same day. It's so hard for me to relax, since there is so much to do." M.W.

"I found out that I was a sane man who dared to take on Time with the thought of squeezing out as much of it as possible. My time follows an inflexible schedule. I normally sleep seven hours, am up by seven and in school from nine to four. From four to ten I'm at work. The most benefit

I've got from the Time homework is the chance to set aside some time to write." H.A.

"After I completed this assignment, I realized how routine my everyday life is. I seem to do the same thing every day at about the same time and for approximately the same time." E.T.

"The exercise of keeping an activity diary made one thing clear—I need more time! It also provided me with an opportunity to reflect on how I spend my time. As a result, I realized how routine my daily activities are, how much time I spend waiting and commuting. For example, I have to wait on line to buy subway tokens, wait for the train, wait for the elevator, wait for the Xerox machine, wait on line at the school registrar and bursar, . . . I also realized that most of my productive time is spent on the job."

"Another important observation is that my thoughts need to be harnessed. It is as though I have no control; one minute I'm thinking about this project while in the next second, I'm onto something totally remote." A.M.

"God, I wish I could use time more efficiently. If only there were a few more extra hours to the day. I have to be on time to classes, to my job, travel and so on. I find myself listening to the loud, clicking sound of my watch. Doing this journal helped me realize just how I spend my time. It was great to slow down for a change and record my thoughts. My life is so full and so rushed that I often lose perspective on how to relax and enjoy it." Y.B.

"I noticed a trend that I broke the day down into blocks: morning, afternoon and evening. I also noticed that I wrote more about things that happened during the day rather than evening. Most of the time periods related to school and work." Z.L.

B. Assignment #5: Apportion Your Time To Meet Your Deadline

As with almost all research, your family history enterprise is limited in scope, e.g., three generations: you and a parent and grandparent of your sex. It's also limited in time: one semester with about 45 hours of class meetings, plus several hours for interviews and library work. This spans 15 weeks, 3 of them already used for preparations. Having already become aware of assignments yet to be completed in the workbook, you have to decide how to apportion the remaining weeks to produce a tentatively near-final draft. You may choose to continue working in your family history after the class ends. Once you ascertain the deadline for your completed draft, you might find it easier to pace yourself.

Some comments from previous students about how they apportioned their time to meet the deadline:

"I divided my time in such a way that 3 weeks were spent on my own history, collecting all information I could from home through interviews, photos, documents, etc. and library work. I spent 3 weeks on my mother's history and the following 3 weeks on my maternal grandmother. This left enough time to put together the histories of all 3, compare them, and polish my final draft." V.R.

"Although I'm not happy with my final history and plan to work on it some more during the summer, I think I was able to plan O.K. I felt rushed because I also work part-time after school. It was also frustrating because I would have preferred to put in a lot more of my own time, but I have a better idea now of how to block out time for a given project." A.W.

C. Assignment #6: Summarizing events, issues and insights in your generation.

A generation constitutes the total population born and living during the same time. There's general agreement that a span of 20 to 25 years extends between birth of parents and birth of offspring.

This assignment is to prepare a 4 to 6 page written (for orientation) account of the significant events that occurred in *your* generation globally, nationally and locally.

(1) *Step 1—Class discussion:*

Begin with class discussion where you jot down in your looseleaf book whatever facts and events occur to you and your classmates that have helped you characterize the times you are living in. Don't be dismayed by scanty knowledge of details, specific dates, or chronology. Instead, look to the class discussion to provide you with a grasp of the period, perhaps stimulating better recall. You might choose to think in categories of events, e.g., WORLD (political, economic, environmental, scientific); NATIONAL (political, social, technological, educational; and LOCAL (social, environmental, cultural). WORLD events might include acts of terrorism, oil spills, droughts, wars, earthquakes, acid rain, emergence of the AIDS virus. National? In 1969, U.S. astronauts' landing on the moon, the first heart transplant, first in-vitro births, sperm banks founded, legal practice of abortion, buying and selling drugs (crack) and human embryos, miniskirts, xerox, word-processors, compact discs, etc. LOCAL events concern mainly state and city, along with neighborhood happenings, e.g., state fairs, elections, emergence of a local magazine, sports club, newspaper or celebrity, special conventions, tragic accidents, crimes, etc.

Posing questions might be helpful, e.g.,

What is the impact of drug-use on our neighborhoods?

Which personalities, aside from family and acquaintances, were conspicuous during your lifetime? Why?

What were some conspicuous conflicts and issues internationally and nationally?

(2) *Step 2—Homework:*

Having compiled your notes in class, the next task is to organize things chronologically and provide details, i.e., library research. A good source is Lois Gordon's and Alan Gordon's, *Six Decades in American Life: 1920–1980.* (Atheneum, N.Y., 1987)

Continue working with your looseleaf, noting precise references for all excerpts, phrases or passages, i.e., exact quotations, page number, author, title, publisher and date of publication. Add whatever other events you may recall while doing the above.

(3) *Step 3—Library Work:*

When ready, start writing your summary. Don't try to include all the events on your list. Your summary should total about 4 to 6 pages and will later serve as a framework for your own personal history. When completed, file your copy in your folder and go on to the next assignment.

D. Assignment #7: Summarizing events, issues and insights in your parents' generation.

(1) *Step 1—Library Work:*

Again, for orientation: library research into the significant events of global, national and local import during your parents' generation. Issues during their youth revolved around bewildering and rapid economic fluctuations, technological advances and international conflicts especially with the Soviet Union following World War II, and the Holocaust. Among other major events were the Korean War, McCarthyism and witch-hunting, the New Frontier of President Kennedy, Peace Corps, Vista, the Great Society of President L. Johnson, the first moon landing by U.S.A. astronauts, the Vietnam War, student sit-ins, assassinations of leaders, etc.[7]

(2) *Step 2—Class discussion:*

Having assembled your data, you may be ready to bring it to class for discussion. Some of you whose parents immigrated to the United States have the task of identifying national and local events in their respective homeland which may have motivated their emigration. A good resource person for help here is your local or school librarian.

If things work out, class discussion may enlarge your understanding of that period—perhaps serving as a dress-rehearsal for sharpening questions when interviewing your parents; for starters, here are a few:

What were women's choices for a lifetime career in your parents' lifetime?

To what do the following terms and names refer and why: "ration cards," "Rosie, the riveter," "Redbaiting," "Cold War," Korea, Martin Luther King, Malcolm X, Civil Rights, Vietnam War, Ed Sullivan, Frank Sinatra, Pearl Bailey, The Beatles, Woodstock, etc.?

Why are your parents likely to recognize these names? Generals Douglas MacArthur, Dwight D. Eisenhower, Admiral Chester Nimitz; Presidents F.D. Roosevelt, Harry S. Truman and John F. Kennedy.

Did other prominent people during your parents' generation influence them? How?

Before and during World War II, 6 million Jews plus many gypsies and political dissidents were murdered in Germany in Adolf Hitler's death camps. Ask your parents to explain, if unlikely to be unbearably painful.

Did these terms mean something to your parents in their youth? CIA, NATO, VISA, McDonalds, Ms., VCR, Rock, Jazz, Swing, supermarkets, condos, pantyhose, the pill, polio shots, penicillin, antibiotics, open-heart surgery, hair transplants, nylons, dacrons, ball point pens, retirees, Golden Agers, Divorcees, nursing homes, microwaves, frozen foods, instant coffee, permanent press clothes, computers, word-processors, laser surgery?

What goals did most people in your parents' generation (male and female) pursue? How much formal schooling did these demand?

---

[7]Lois & A. Gordon's *Six Decades in American Life: 1920–1980,* (Atheneum, N.Y., 1987) R.D. Marcus & D. Burner, editors, *America Since 1945,* 3rd Edition, (N.Y.: St. Martin's Press, 1981)

John Dos Passos, *State Of The Nation* (Westport, Ct. Greenwood Press, 1973) A. Lewis, *Portrait Of A Decade: The Second American Revolution* (N.Y.: Random House, 1964)

Carruth, Gordon, *The Encyclopedia Of American Facts and Dates* Eighth Edition (N.Y. Harper and Row, 1987)

How common was it for unmarried children to leave home in your parents' generation. Why did they do it?

Doubtless further questions will come up during the discussion. Jot 'em down and, keep them handy for quick reference.

(3) *Step 3—homework:*

Ask your parents for an appointment to interview them. Since this, perhaps, will be the first of several interviews with them, and since this first interview is not ostensibly geared to elicit personal information it might be appropriate to suggest that they also invite one or more of their contemporaries. Explain beforehand the reason for the interview. Don't neglect to ask permission to take notes, especially for using direct quotes and/or a tape recorder. This of course applies to whomever they may invite.

During the interview narrow your talk as much as possible to questions about issues and events in their youth. In thereby disclosing your care in preparation, your parents and their friends may be encouraged to full, even enthusiastic participation.

(4) *Step 4—Homework:*

After you've collected this raw material, and condensed it into a 4 to 6 page summary, file it in the folder earmarked for your parent.

E. Assignment #8: Summarizing events, issues and insights during your grandparents' generation.

(1) *Step 1—Library Research:*

In recording major events and issues during your grandparents' generation, begin soon after World War I, e.g., 65 to 75 years ago. As previously noted, male students should limit research to the paternal side, females to the maternal. As noted, those whose grandparents emigrated from different countries, or are deceased, or reachable only by phone can get most of the information for this assignment from library sources and interviews with survivors of the period.

Try to imagine an even greater contrast between life-styles in your grandparents' generation and your own than that between yours and your parents'. The revolutionary changes set in motion before the turn of the century intensified in the developing cities of eastern U.S.A.: the need grew for cheap, semi-skilled manual labor, especially keen were needs born from the vast industrialization stimulated by much immigration during and soon after the Civil War.

During World War I, outbreak of a devastating epidemic—Spanish influenza—aroused public demand for far-reaching public health reforms. Many, including perhaps your grandparents, continued to be lured from their farms by promises of land or other glowing opportunities in a new country. Forsaking their centuries-old traditional work as farmers and craftsmen, many became factory workers, miners, mechanics, and day laborers, skipping the traditional long apprenticeships. Cottage industries dependent on skilled manual time-consuming labor were replaced by mass production, manufacturing and distribution by rail. Travel by horse and buggy became a sentimental relic of the past as railroads, automobiles, airplanes increased mobility. The national landscape was laced with ribbons of tracks and concrete roads. Soon bloody protests between labor and management gave rise to labor unions which only gained real power with the advent of Franklin Roosevelt's New Deal. Also, as electricity came into widespread use, many enjoyed for the first time the once luxury of indoor plumbing and refrigeration. Widespread reforms resulted: better sanitation, housing, and working conditions. Improved access to vital information, entertainment through newspapers, magazines, radio and movies eased acquiring knowledge on how to enter the mainstream of American life. Then came the devastating economic collapse of the 1930s: the Great Depression. Breadlines, migrant-workers,[8] dance marathons,[9] Hollywood escapist extravaganzas and soon after, radio comedies joined with experimental government programs (WPA, NRA, CCC) to make conditions bearable until these measures began to work. Outbreak of World War II in 1939 awakened America's consciousness of their prized freedoms as news of the Nazi atrocities trickled back from Germany of the holocaust. Such are only a smidgin of the cataclysms and confusions of your near-ancestor's era.

(2) *Step 2—Class Discussion:*

For enlivening class discussion of this era, you may wish to consider the following questions:

Drugs (Crack and Marijuana) are a serious national threat today. With what habit-forming drugs were your grandparents preoccupied?

This generation is much concerned with the issues of abortion and the death penalty. Were these similar issues in your grandparents' day?

How important was mother in your grandparents' era?

---

[8]See John Steinbeck's, *The Grapes Of Wrath* (N.Y. Modern Library, 1939)

[9]Film entitled: *They Shoot Horses, Don't They?* starring Jane Fonda U.S.: Sydney Pollack, 1969. Based on the novel of the same name by Horace McCoy in 1935

In your grandparents' generation, what career choices other than homemakers did women have?

What were your grandparents' attitudes toward sex and moving out of the home before marriage?

Besides the Lindberg baby kidnapping—a notorious crime that occurred in grandparents' time,—what other notorious crimes took place?

Who were the dominant personalities then? Why?

What other sources of entertainment were there besides radio and pool halls?

Who were the favorite entertainers and movie stars of the period?

What important medical and scientific discoveries took place at this time?

What home remedies for illness or injuries did your grandparents rely on?

If you were to make up a shopping list for food, clothing, and household appliances, what items would you include and where would you be likely to purchase them in that era?

If any one of your grandparents emigrated from another country, what kinds of painful adjustments might they have had to make?

As before, do take notes in your looseleaf during the discussion, providing as well as asking in return from your classmates as many details and documentation as possible. Fill in gaps with further library research.

(3) *Step 3—Homework:*

As arranged earlier with your parents and their contemporaries, set about to interview your grandparents and/or survivor(s) of their generation. Explain, as objectively yet warmly as you can, your aim and ask permission to take notes, and/or to tape-record. The same instructions apply as those for interviewing your parents.

(4) *Step 4—Homework:*

Boil down your data into a 4 to 6 page summary; file it in the folder earmarked ''grandparent'' and tackle the next step.

Chapter Five

Assembling Family-History Data

Congratulations! Boiling down and organizing such a formidable mass of raw information concerning three generations—including your own—wasn't simple.

This sort of family-history research began at a fixed span of time, i.e., your generation, and proceeded backwards to span two more generations—about 75 years. However limited in *time,* its *scope* began on a global scale yet, of necessity, must focus on the personal histories of 3 individual family members, each belonging to his/her respective generation. Accordingly, again, you must tap the same two sources, i.e., (1) primary (statistical) data from official documents plus eye-witness accounts through interviews; and (2) secondary sources (descriptive and/or anecdotal).

The idea is to help you see yourself and parents *and* grandparents as more-or-less representative people within their era. If needed, add blank pages to your looseleaf. Divide these, as before, into three roughly equal sections: the first third for notes on *Self;* the second third on *Mother/Father;* the last on *Maternal Grandmother/Paternal Grandfather.* To avoid smearing copy use a not-too-soft pencil, (#2 is standard).

Start with your own personal history along these guidelines:

(1) Fill in detailed guide-sheets

(2) Answer open-ended questionnaire

(3) Summarize information from both sources'

(4) Summarize your comparison from the detailed guide-sheets of the 3 generations.

A. Assignment #9

(1) *Fill in Detailed Guide-sheets on Self*
Transfer as much information onto these as you can find around your home, from all manner of certificates, announcements, school records, diplomas, awards, picture postcards, social security cards, driver's licenses, wage and rent receipts (charts in Chapter Three—pages 22 to 30—provide further likely sources, along with addresses to write to replace important missing documents—birth certificates, evidence of citizenship and military discharges). For further help in obtaining a document ask your instructor or librarian. Since questions in categories VI, VII and VIII may not apply to you, skip them or simply write N.A. (non-applicable). Accuracy of detail can prove important in ways yet unforseeable, so copy, exactly as recorded, names, dates, titles of documents, dates of publication and page number on which the information appears. Please be concise. If space for answers in a category on the guidesheet isn't enough, add and number another blank sheet from your looseleaf. You may unexpectedly later recall an incident or two so have your notebook as accessible as possible.
(2) *Please answer open-ended questionnaire*
Continuing with *Self,* answer as many of the open-ended questions you can (see end of this section), and write them into your looseleaf in the appropriate section. You'll note that several questions appear under each category on the questionnaire. These categories align with the categories listed on the detailed guidesheets. Almost all the information asked for on the detailed guidesheets is statistical and/or quantitative. Not so the open-ended questions which are intended to elicit information not available from documents, and may be rather subjective and mainly descriptive. All of us select what we remember. Often and unconsciously we may distort important details of an experience or anecdote. However superb one's memory it's a very good idea for cross-checking by interviewing family and friends who lived through the same events. With whatever tact you can summon, remind them of your task, set up a mutually convenient (semi-formal perhaps) appointment and, as before, ask permission to take notes and/or tape-

record. Should any interviewees ask to see the final write-up and you promise to show it, do keep the promise.

Skip questions that don't apply. Where needed, include data from your detailed guidesheets. What is wanted is content and continuity built on facts: an accurate, chronological and, at times, analytical recounting of your (and later, your mother's/father's, maternal grandmother's, paternal grandfather's) life. For the sake of manageability, tackle only one category at a time and answer one question at a time. It is neither necessary nor desirable to include every incident or event that comes to mind: selectivity is the aim. Strive for simple sentences salting in, now and then, an occasional telling observation and/or direct quote. Acknowledge these with footnotes giving time(s) and date(s) of interview(s), plus name(s) of people interviewed. It may be desirable at times to so combine questions as to elicit a single answer, e.g.,

Category #1—Question 1: When were you born?
Question 2: Where were you born?

Answer: I was born on July 10th, 1972, in Jersey City, New Jersey

Don't suppose you must answer every question. Here's where judgement, however inescapably subjective, may yield clues about a person's preferences, cherished memory, values and, perhaps, a unique trait, e.g.,

Category #1—Question 3: Do you remember your first home?

Answer: It was a two-story, single-family brick dwelling with a one-car garage to one side and a small garden in back where my father grew vegetables and mother had a garden patch. Often in childhood she surprised with a small bouquet of flowers in my bedroom.

(3) *Summarize information from both sources*
When you've answered all questions on the detailed guidesheets, also the open-ended questionnaire, you'll probably have more than enough information from which to draw on for a preliminary account of your history. Had you adhered to the earlier suggestion to answer questions in sentence form, you will be agreeably surprised to find that

much was already written down. All that may be needed might be a little condensing or slight revision. It may run to 10 to 15 pages, perhaps more. Whether short or long, it should truthfully sketch high points in your history.

B. Assignment #10

(1) Fill in detailed guidesheets for mother/father with their cooperation.

(2) Interview mother/father and, if necessary, one or more of their contemporaries for answers to open-ended questionnaire.

OPEN-ENDED INTERVIEW QUESTIONNAIRE

In the following questions, the word "you" refers to the one being interviewed.

I. *Basic Information*

When were you born?
Where were you born?
Do you remember your first home? Neighborhood? Town?
How many times has your family moved, including before your
    birth?
When did you (or family) move to your present residence?

II. *Siblings*

How many brothers and sisters have you?
Have they (and you) nicknames?
To which brother or sister were you closest? Why? As a child,
    with whom did you play most often, if outside the family?
Can you remember the birthdays of all your siblings? What were
    your favorite childhood games and stories? What family activ-
    ity did you prize as a child?

III. *School*

How many years of formal schooling have you had up to now?
Did expectations for formal education differ in your family for
    boys and girls?

What unique skills, talent and/or disability did you possess from early on, and how did it affect you?

Did you receive any specialized training outside of formal schooling? (music, art, religious or non-English language lessons?)

IV. *Record of Paid Employment*

Were family members (either sex) expected to earn money?

What guided occupational choices for males? For females?

In your generation, what were the attitudes toward women working outside the home?

Do you recall your first weekly wage? Working conditions?

Has there been a change in total number of weekly work hours?

Was Social Security implemented in your lifetime?

V. *Leisure Time Activities*

Did you have to visit family members on specific occasions, i.e., holidays and/or summer vacations?

What family social functions did you attend?

Did religion affect the way you were brought up?

Have you traveled much? Where and How?

What kind of entertainment do you prefer?

Have you any special hobbies?

How much reading do you do?

VI. *Marriage*

How did you meet your husband/wife?

How far away from you did your spouse live while you were courting?

Can you tell me about your courtship?

What decided you to marry?

How old were you at marriage?

(To be asked only of immigrants to the U.S.) In general, could you describe the differences you found in America re. mate-selection, courtship and marriage as compared with the old country?

What were the prevailing attitudes in your generation toward divorce and marriage?

Is there a sharp age difference between you and spouse?

Did you and spouse agree before marriage about the number of children you would have?

Did a cultural and/or religious similarity influence your choice of marriage partner?

Did a cultural and/or religious practice influence your choice of names for your children?

VII. *Military experience*

Were you ever drafted? Did you volunteer for military service?

How long did you serve?

How old were you at the time?

Was any specialized training involved?

Have you photographs of yourself in uniform?

What are some memorable service experiences?

Was it war time?

Did you see combat?

Were you wounded? Decorated?

What was your family's attitude toward your decision to enlist (if you enlisted)?

Are you glad you enlisted?

Do you feel your military experience helped/hindered your future in any way?

VIII. *Affiliations*

Do you participate in any religious/social/political organizations?

Are you a member of a professional organization(s)?

Do you hold office in any religious/social/political and professional organization?

Were you born in a country other than the U.S.A.?

Can you recall the date, time, manner of departure and the length of time your trip took to reach U.S.A.?

Are you a U.S. citizen?

Do you belong to a particular ethnic organization?

Have you membership in a fraternity/sorority?

What charitable organizations do you most admire?

IX. *Generational Materials*

Who were your favorite entertainers? (singers, dancers, etc.)

Who were your favorite artists? (authors, painters, musicians)

Who were your favorite sports figures?
Have you any favorite culture hero/heroine in government, politics, education, science, finance, etc?
Can you recall the first U.S. president for whom you voted?
How many things can you think of that have been invented since your childhood?
What major global and/or national event do you recall that occurred in earlier years? Did it affect you and/or your family? How?

X. *Health Profile*

Have you any particular food favorites? Any you dislike? Allergic to?
Did you suffer the common childhood illnesses? Any additional ones? Did one in particular affect your life? How?
What is the lifespan pattern of your family for the past 3 or more generations?
What has been the most frequent cause of death among family members?
Is there particular disease or affliction that has affected more than one generation of a family member?
Are you diet conscious? Your parents? Grandparents?
Would you describe yourself as a physically active person?

XI. *Family Anecdotes, Proverbs, Legends, Stories, etc.*

Do you recall any favorite family proverbs?
Do you recall any favorite family stories or anecdotes?
How about family superstitions?
What are some favorite family traditions?
Were there any particular family tragedies?
Was there a "black sheep" in your family? A family hero? A family heroine?

C. Assignment #11

DETAILED GUIDESHEET: SELF (MALE/FEMALE)
cross out one

I. *DATE OF BIRTH:*

Place of birth _____
Time of birth (if known) _____
Geographic location (proximity to what city?) _____
Climate; environmental features noted? _____

II. *NUMBER OF SIBLINGS:*

Younger than you _____   No. yrs. younger: _____
Older than you _____   No. yrs. older: _____
Any half-sisters? _____   Age of half sister _____
    step-sisters _____   Age of step sister _____
Any death of sibling(s) _____   Age(s) at death(s) _____

III. *SCHOOL*

Name & location of school(s) in order of attendance _____
_____
Year graduated from Grammar School _____
Year graduated from Jr. High School _____
Year graduated from High School _____
Type of course in High School (Secretarial, College prep.?)
_____
Any skill courses? _____
Special skill training? _____

IV. *RECORD OF PAID EMPLOYMENT*

Age at first employment _____
Hourly wage _____   Weekly wage: _____
No. hrs. worked daily _____   (weekly) _____
Type of work _____
No. of jobs held _____
Any special training or skills learned on job _____
_____
Occupation _____
Profession _____
Types of diplomas and degrees _____

V. *LEISURE-TIME ACTIVITIES*

Skills _____
Hobbies _____
Membership(s) in organizations (religious, social, professional,
    etc.) _____
Number of types of vacations _____
Amount of travel (States visited, countries, etc.) _____

VI. *MARRIAGE*

Age at marriage ————————————————————
Total number of years married to same spouse ——————
Total number of marriages ——————————————————
Spouse's occupation and age ————————————————

VII. *NUMBER OF CHILDREN:* (Total)

In order of birth:
Name ————————————— Birthdate: ——————————
————————————— ——————————
————————————— ——————————

Death(s) Name(s)/Date/Cause
————————————————————————————————
————————————————————————————————

SECOND MARRIAGE:
Spouse's name & Age: ————————————————————
Name & Age of Children: ————————————————
————————————————————————————————

VIII. *MILITARY EXPERIENCE*

Dates/Rank/No. Yrs. ——————————————————————
Assignments (Location) ——————————————————
Awards ——————————————————————————————
Date & Type of discharge ————————————————

IX. *AFFILIATIONS*

Religious ——————————————————————————————
Political ————————————————————————————————
Immigration dates: departure place ——— arrival place ———
Citizenship (Present) ——————————————————————
Ethnic (nationality)/or Racial ————————————————

X. *GENERATIONAL MATERIAL*

Agricultural Age _____
  Victorian? _____
Industrial Age _____
Atomic Age _____
Space Age _____
Wars/Inventions/Discoveries _____
U.S. Presidents, _____ year birth to present?: _____
Favorite Personalities _____, Actors, Writers, Scientists,
  Athletes
Favorite Songs, Symphonies, Concertos _____
Musicals, Operas and Composers _____
Painters _____
Plays & Playwrights _____
Statesmen (Politicians) _____

XI. *HEALTH PROFILE*

Common childhood diseases: _____
Any prolonged illness _____
Accident _____
Inherited affliction, e.g., diabetes, M.S., etc. _____
Death(s) of grandparent(s) _____ (age)
_____ (causes)

XII. *FAMILY ANECDOTES, PROVERBS, LEGENDS, STORIES*
(These are usually passed down by word-of-mouth)

DETAILED GUIDESHEET: MOTHER/FATHER cross out one

I. *DATE OF BIRTH:*

Place of birth _____
Time of birth (if known) _____
Geographic location (proximity to what city?) _____
Climate; environmental features noted? _____

II. *NUMBER OF SIBLINGS:*

Younger than you _____	No. yrs. younger: _____
Older than you _____	No. yrs. older: _____
Any half-sisters? _____	Age of half sister _____
step-sisters _____	Age of step sister _____
Any death of sibling(s) _____	Age(s) at death(s) _____

III. *SCHOOL*

Name & location of school(s) in order of attendance _____

_____

Year graduated from Grammar School _____
Year graduated from Jr. High School _____
Year graduated from High School _____
Type of course in High School (Secretarial, College prep.?)

_____

Any skill courses? _____
Special skill training? _____

IV. *RECORD OF PAID EMPLOYMENT*

Age at first employment _____
Hourly wage _____ Weekly wage: _____
No. hrs. worked daily _____ (weekly) _____
Type of work _____
No. of jobs held _____
Any special training or skills learned on job _____

_____

Occupation _____
Profession _____
Types of diplomas and degrees _____

V. *LEISURE-TIME ACTIVITIES*

Skills _____
Hobbies _____
Membership(s) in organizations (religious, social, professional,
    etc.) _____
Number of types of vacations _____
Amount of travel (States visited, countries, etc.) _____

VI. *MARRIAGE*

Age at marriage _____
Total number of years married to same spouse _____
Total number of marriages _____
Spouse's occupation and age _____

VII. *NUMBER OF CHILDREN:* (Total)
        In order of birth:
            Name _____   Birthdate: _____
                    _____   _____
                    _____   _____

        Death(s) Name(s)/Date/Cause
        _____
        _____

        SECOND MARRIAGE:
            Spouse's name & Age: _____
            Name & Age of Children: _____
                    _____

VIII. *MILITARY EXPERIENCE*

        Dates/Rank/No. Yrs. _____
        Assignments (Location) _____
        Awards _____
        Date & Type of discharge _____

IX. *AFFILIATIONS*

        Religious _____
        Political _____
            Immigration dates: departure place _____ arrival place _____
            Citizenship (Present) _____
            Ethnic (nationality)/or Racial _____

X. *GENERATIONAL MATERIAL*

        Agricultural Age _____
            Victorian? _____
        Industrial Age _____
        Atomic Age _____
        Space Age _____
        Wars/Inventions/Discoveries _____
        U.S. Presidents, _____ year birth to present?: _____
        Favorite Personalities _____, Actors, Writers, Scientists,
            Athletes
        Favorite Songs, Symphonies, Concertos _____
        Musicals, Operas and Composers _____
        Painters _____
        Plays & Playwrights _____
        Statesmen (Politicians) _____

XI. *HEALTH PROFILE*

Common childhood diseases: _____
Any prolonged illness _____
Accident _____
Inherited affliction, e.g., diabetes, M.S., etc. _____
Death(s) of grandparent(s) _____ (age)
_____ (causes)

XII. *FAMILY ANECDOTES, PROVERBS, LEGENDS, STORIES*
(These are usually passed down by word-of-mouth)

DETAILED GUIDESHEET: MATERNAL GRANDMOTHER/
PATERNAL GRANDFATHER cross out one

I. *DATE OF BIRTH:*

Place of birth _____
Time of birth (if known) _____
Geographic location (proximity to what city?) _____
Climate; environmental features noted? _____

II. *NUMBER OF SIBLINGS:*

Younger than you _____ No. yrs. younger: _____
Older than you _____ No. yrs. older: _____
Any half-sisters? _____ Age of half sister _____
    step-sisters _____ Age of step sister _____
Any death of sibling(s) _____ Age(s) at death(s) _____

III. *SCHOOL*

Name & location of school(s) in order of attendance _____

_____
Year graduated from Grammar School _____
Year graduated from Jr. High School _____
Year graduated from High School _____
Type of course in High School (Secretarial, College prep.?)

_____
Any skill courses? _____
Special skill training? _____

IV. *RECORD OF PAID EMPLOYMENT*

Age at first employment _____

Hourly wage _____ Weekly wage: _____

No. hrs. worked daily _____ (weekly) _____

Type of work _____

No. of jobs held _____

Any special training or skills learned on job _____

_____

Occupation _____

Profession _____

Types of diplomas and degrees _____

V. *LEISURE-TIME ACTIVITIES*

Skills _____

Hobbies _____

Membership(s) in organizations (religious, social, professional, etc.) _____

Number of types of vacations _____

Amount of travel (States visited, countries, etc.) _____

VI. *MARRIAGE*

Age at marriage _____

Total number of years married to same spouse _____

Total number of marriages _____

Spouse's occupation and age _____

VII. *NUMBER OF CHILDREN:* (Total)

In order of birth:

Name _____ Birthdate: _____

_____ _____

_____ _____

Death(s) Name(s)/Date/Cause

_____

_____

SECOND MARRIAGE:

Spouse's name & Age: _____

Name & Age of Children: _____

_____

VIII. *MILITARY EXPERIENCE*

Dates/Rank/No. Yrs. ⎯⎯⎯⎯⎯⎯⎯⎯⎯⎯⎯⎯⎯⎯⎯
Assignments (Location) ⎯⎯⎯⎯⎯⎯⎯⎯⎯⎯⎯⎯
Awards ⎯⎯⎯⎯⎯⎯⎯⎯⎯⎯⎯⎯⎯⎯⎯⎯⎯⎯⎯⎯
Date & Type of discharge ⎯⎯⎯⎯⎯⎯⎯⎯⎯⎯⎯

IX. *AFFILIATIONS*

Religious ⎯⎯⎯⎯⎯⎯⎯⎯⎯⎯⎯⎯⎯⎯⎯⎯⎯⎯
Political ⎯⎯⎯⎯⎯⎯⎯⎯⎯⎯⎯⎯⎯⎯⎯⎯⎯⎯⎯
   Immigration dates: departure place ⎯⎯ arrival place ⎯⎯
   Citizenship (Present) ⎯⎯⎯⎯⎯⎯⎯⎯⎯⎯⎯⎯
   Ethnic (nationality)/or Racial ⎯⎯⎯⎯⎯⎯⎯⎯⎯

X. *GENERATIONAL MATERIAL*

Agricultural Age ⎯⎯ ⎯⎯⎯⎯⎯⎯⎯⎯⎯⎯⎯⎯
   Victorian? ⎯⎯⎯⎯⎯⎯⎯⎯⎯⎯⎯⎯⎯⎯⎯⎯
Industrial Age ⎯⎯⎯⎯⎯⎯⎯⎯⎯⎯⎯⎯⎯⎯⎯
Atomic Age ⎯⎯⎯⎯⎯⎯⎯⎯⎯⎯⎯⎯⎯⎯⎯⎯
Space Age ⎯⎯⎯⎯⎯⎯⎯⎯⎯⎯⎯⎯⎯⎯⎯⎯
Wars/Inventions/Discoveries ⎯⎯⎯⎯⎯⎯⎯⎯⎯⎯
U.S. Presidents, ⎯⎯⎯⎯⎯ year birth to present?: ⎯⎯⎯⎯
Favorite Personalities ⎯⎯⎯⎯⎯, Actors, Writers, Scientists,
   Athletes
Favorite Songs, Symphonies, Concertos ⎯⎯⎯⎯⎯⎯⎯
Musicals, Operas and Composers ⎯⎯⎯⎯⎯⎯⎯⎯
Painters ⎯⎯⎯⎯⎯⎯⎯⎯⎯⎯⎯⎯⎯⎯⎯⎯⎯⎯
Plays & Playwrights ⎯⎯⎯⎯⎯⎯⎯⎯⎯⎯⎯⎯⎯
Statesmen (Politicians) ⎯⎯⎯⎯⎯⎯⎯⎯⎯⎯⎯⎯

XI. *HEALTH PROFILE*

Common childhood diseases: ⎯⎯⎯⎯⎯⎯⎯⎯⎯⎯
Any prolonged illness ⎯⎯⎯⎯⎯⎯⎯⎯⎯⎯⎯⎯⎯
Accident ⎯⎯⎯⎯⎯⎯⎯⎯⎯⎯⎯⎯⎯⎯⎯⎯⎯⎯
Inherited affliction, e.g., diabetes, M.S., etc. ⎯⎯⎯⎯⎯
Death(s) of grandparent(s) ⎯⎯⎯⎯⎯⎯⎯⎯⎯⎯ (age)
⎯⎯⎯⎯⎯⎯⎯⎯⎯⎯⎯⎯⎯⎯⎯⎯⎯⎯⎯ (causes)

XII. *FAMILY ANECDOTES, PROVERBS, LEGENDS, STORIES*
(These are usually passed down by word-of-mouth)

D. Assignment #12

Transfer the information you've already gathered and recorded from the Detailed Guidesheets for each Representative of the 3 generations to the Comparative Analysis of Data form.

E. Assignment #13

Compare the data from each category on the Comparative Analysis of Data form, record your conclusion in your looseleaf. For example, an answer to Category I may reveal that your grandparent was born in a single-family house, perhaps in another country, and that she grew up in a country town, but you may've been born in a city apartment and grew up in a metropolitan area.

Category II (family size) may trace a trend from large family in your grandparent's generation (7 to 10 siblings), to a small family in your parent's generation (3 to 6 siblings), and an even smaller one in your generation (1 to 3).

Category III (# yrs. formal schooling) may show a trend towards clearly more years devoted to formal schooling from your grandparent's generation to yours.

Category IV (age at first employment, hourly wage, etc.), you may be surprised to learn of the many contrasts.

Write down your findings the best you can, then bring them to class for discussion. Add afterthoughts, if any, then summarize all at home and file your conclusions (4 to 6 pages) in the folder marked: *Analysis of Data For 3 Generations*.

COMPARATIVE ANALYSIS OF DATA FOR 3 GENERATIONS
MATERNAL/PATERNAL LINE (Cross Out One)

	Gr. Mother Gr. Father	Mother Father	Self Female/Male
I. *DATE OF BIRTH PLACE, ETC.* TOWN: CITY: COUNTRY: CLIMATE:			
II. No. of Siblings Younger—Older of Half Siblings of Step Siblings			
III. No. Yrs. Formal Schooling (Total)			
IV. *Record of Paid Employment* Age At First Employment Hourly Wage: No. of Hrs. Required Daily Weekly Wage: # of Hrs. Required Weekly Occupation/Type of position			
V. Leisure-time Activities: Skills ——————— Hobbies —————— Membership in Organizations Communication Facilities Technology (Electricity, Steam, etc. # and Type Vacation Amt. Travel)			
VI. Age at Marriage: Age of Marriage Total # Yrs. Married to First Spouse No. of Marriages;			
VII. Total No. Children Born: Total No. Children Died: Age(s) at Death Cause(s) of Death Total No. Half Children			
VIII. Military Experience Date of Enlistment or Draft Rank No. Yrs. Served Assigned Location(s) Awards Date & Type Discharge			

	Gr. Mother Gr. Father	Mother Father	Self Female/Male

IX. Affiliations:
    Religious
    Political
        Immigration Date
        Departure Place
        Arrival Place & Date
        Citizenship
            (Present)
    Ethnic
        Nationality
        Racial			

Chapter Six

Environmental Influences— Physical and Human— On One's Life and Personality

Most of the information you've assembled was to answer WHAT happened, WHEN, WHERE and, in particular to WHOM, i.e., yourself, parent, and grandparent. Now for the HOW by which such happenings shaped one's life and personality.

Dissecting out causes and effects in formation of one's personality can be tricky. One's personality is obviously and somehow mysteriously shaped by the interplay of genes and temperament with the cultural and human environments one is born into, and superimposed vivid life experiences. Introspection, however occasionally painful, on the influences of these factors on yourself, parent and grandparent, may foster charity and understanding.

We start with class discussion. Please bring to class your materials: historical summaries, guidesheets, comparative analysis sheets, loose-leaf notes, and copies of official documents; include photographs. Use copies of official documents to avoid losing the originals. In class discussions information may overlap; nevertheless, try to stick to each of the following:

1—Physical environment
2—Human (cultural) environment
    a. Effects of inherited physical make-up, cultural attributions and self-perception
    b. Effects of decisive and crucial life experiences

1. The Physical Environment

For health, an organism must adapt to its physical environment; in the current language of physiology and biochemistry, it must adapt to stress. How it happens is sometimes mysterious. Humans get most information from eyes and ears. A dog relies primarily on its nose and eyes. It sees or smells danger. Humans respond to their environment through all senses—touch, taste, sight, sound, smell and mechanisms of self-awareness to know that, at least, one's muscles are ready for fight or flight. We respond in various ways, some learned, some spontaneous. We are born with perhaps only a few rigidly channeled instincts. From birth onwards we learn and learn until death.

All multicellular animals have a brain or recognizable equivalent; ours is among the most complex. Other forms respond mainly stereotypically to environmental challenge; our elaborate neural network enables us to learn to manipulate the environment in ways favoring survival. We have no say as to *where* to be born (let alone *when*), but one's birthplace shapes as well as limits the ways to meet those challenges. The French relish horse meat; Chinese eat dog; Australian aborigines eat insect grubs; others eat termites or grasshoppers. People are selected in short and long terms for eating what in the environment favors survival. The physical environment, too, influences what is acceptable behavior. If your paternal grandfather had been born on a farm, he learned to wake at dawn then do the necessary farm chores. If born in Finland, Norway or Switzerland your maternal grandmother had to learn early to ski and skate. The climate called for warm clothing and hearty meals. A mountainous environment hardly encouraged swimming and water skiing. People born in the Arctic (Eskimos above all), had to learn to relish blubber, raw fish, seal and whale meat with few if any vegetables and be skilled with harpoon or bow and arrow (lately, too, rifles). Males learned to construct shelters of skins or of snow and ice, and kayaks with animal skins. Wives were skillful sewers. But one born in Bombay wears light cotton garments, cultivates rice and vegetables, little or no meat available, but fish when possible. The Arctic would hardly provide opportunity to surf, nor is ice skating the thing in Bombay.

The environment may inflict typhoons, swarming locusts, earthquakes, mud slides, epidemics, noise from industrial traffic and chemical disasters, as well as the abrasions of domestic overcrowding. Having left their rather sparsely populated rural environments in Europe your grandparents, if emigrating to the United States, abruptly found themselves confronted with disease-carriers assembled from all over the world and against which selection in their homeland had been weak, hence the devastation caused by tuberculosis in Manhattan's Little Italy in the early 1900s.

Further questions to explore:

• In which generation did serious worry about the environment become prevalent? Why?

• What climatic and geographic differences existed for the three generations?

• Identify some of the skills required of each generation to cope with their respective environments.

• What sorts of clothing did the physical environment require of each generation? What fibers or other materials?

• How much more diverse are the foods available to your generation than for the previous two? How come?

• Identify some of the main environmental hazards in each generation and their effect on each of the individuals chosen for your study.

• Has the present physical environment, notably urbanization and industrial scale farming and mass hospitalization, become more challenging than for your grandparents' generation? Why?

• Are you more likely to encounter a greater variety of physical environments (especially through travel for recreation and education) than were your parents and grandparents?

• How have recent cultural developments affected your physical environment, e.g., great increase in the number of cars, buses, trucks, use of fertilizers, sources of electric power and communication devices?

A. Assignment #14

(1) Drawing from your class discussion, summarize—2 to 3 pages— how the *physical* environment into which you were born still affects your life and personality.

(2) Summarize—2 to 3 pages—how the *physical* environment into which your mother/father was born affected her/his life and personality.

(3) Summarize—2 to 3 pages—how the *physical* environment into which your maternal grandmother/paternal grandfather was born affected her/his life and personality.

2. The Cultural Environment

Humans, as primates, depend for survival on other primates; for us it is the family. The enveloping environment you came into—your family—perhaps has affected you the most enduringly. The family names you, toilet trains you; teaches you who's boss, tells you what language to speak; when to say "please" and "thank you," how and what to eat and share, and tells you what to believe. In sum, your family makes you define your identity and more or less prescribes your design for living. This design (pattern, blue-print, life style, manners, etc.) expresses underlying gene similarities and encompasses behavioral similarities through imitation of family ways. Nonetheless these ways affect each family member differently, unless the person is one of identical twins. Each family member is influenced by family size; composition; religion; economic and educational status; political structure of its country; and prevailing attitudes toward race and ethnic background.

Look at the *political* structure where the family lives: is it a democracy, dictatorship or police state, oligarchy or near anarchy? Is at least minimal education available to all or reserved for an elite? Does the observable political structure hinder or promote genuine equality of race and sex? Does covert class prejudice channel employment and promote advancement of a particular group? Is there enough food and housing for all? For example, your grandparents—if born in red Russia shortly after World War I—never experienced the political freedom which their contemporaries in the United States enjoy simply by birth in a reasonably functional democracy. But even democracies may harbor some prejudices against one or another racial or ethnic subgroup. Recall the aforementioned grandmother, born black and poor with several siblings in a Western metropolitan environment peopled mostly by blue-collar whites who disliked nonwhites. Although the grandmother had grown up in a warm, loving family, nevertheless prejudice militated against her enjoying equal opportunities in education and employment and affected her perception of self and the world.

Economic differentials among families may account for size and composition as well as sex determined differences in child-rearing. Poor families—for reasons noted—tended to be large (especially in your grandparents era) and extending to 3, sometimes even 4 generations (widowed grandparent or great-grandparent and, where obligation was felt, in-laws). Male children were early urged to become wage earners at sacrifice of schooling; females were directed—implicitly or openly—towards early marriage and motherhood. Formal *education* beyond elementary school was seldom envisioned, and tolerated only for males. Not so with smaller native-born families consisting of only 2 generations, i.e., nuclear; these are apt to be in less harsh economic circumstances with lessened sex differentiation. Parents were learning to emphasize the higher education needed for professional training for both sexes. Small families prevail in Westernized economies. Chances are you yourself may well be a member of a nuclear family—perhaps only one or two siblings—and live in an urban complex or private suburban house with both parents wage earners. How else might you have been able to spend your vacations at sleep-away camps, traveled widely in your early teens, and acquired your own word-processor, perhaps even a car—all beyond reach of your contemporaries born in a large, somewhat poor family with only one (divorced or widowed) parent. These differential family experiences are likely to be expressed in different feelings about self and others.

Similar surmises could be formulated about the influence of *ethnicity* on personal development. If you were brought up in the United States by native-born parents, your first language would be American-English. But had your parents come from Poland, Italy or Russia soon after your birth, you may have learned their native language first, then had to cope with English in school. You may also have been openly pressured early on by your parents to conform to ethnic family ways— diet, religious observances, choice of friends, school discipline, leisure activities, and behavior towards family including elders. Home discipline may have sought to perpetuate remnants of a ghetto mentality seemingly at odds with the social and cultural patterns encountered in school, job and the world at large. Frustrations and misunderstandings—even agonies—when the two conflict may prompt rebellion not only against parents, but against your ethnic background. You might therefore examine some rationale for your parents' behavior, e.g., isolation felt on their arrival here, hence an indispensable anchor provided by their traditional beliefs and customs as they strove to cope with what was still an alien society, and what they may well have sensed as a widening generative gap with their children which they felt helpless to arrest.

Look at their background. Between 1890 and 1910, the lure of employment opportunities and hope of a better life in the United States led approximately 22 million people from Europe to emigrate, i.e., Italy, Austria-Hungary, Sweden, Finland, Norway, and Russia. Most were peasant farmers or small tradesmen. Many were partly or wholly illiterate in their written language and bewildered by the language and customs of their new country. They took refuge in closeness and helped establish separate ethnic settlements (ghettos) in the cheapest areas of the large cities, where the ordeals of acculturation could be mitigated by friends who had, with some success, preceded them.

Once here, and despite meager resources, the immigrants established their own churches (as did the Pilgrims). Accustomed to gnawing uncertainties in the Old Country, limited in information, beset with peasant cynicisms, e.g., "You can't fight City Hall," they clung to the folkways of the old country with its deep-seated distrust of people outside their extended family (their main insurance policy or safety net).

For centuries the family economy—farming, fishing, hunting and requisite tools and techniques—had remained much the same. The family harvest and/or herds had always been subject to the whims of weather, market and remote, sometimes ruthless overlords. Most children died before age ten; many adults became widowed before the tenth year of marriage. No wonder that their prime trust was in the family. Barter and gift exchanges kept the kinship group functional, preventing a member of one family from cheating a member of another, or committing any disgraceful act, including defaulting on one's debts. Since family members lived in poverty dictated proximity, the behavior of each was easily monitored. Privacy was minimal. The competent elderly were matter-of-factly called upon to baby-sit and otherwise help the young. Where possible in the old country, farms were held intact and passed from father to eldest son, notably among the Irish and Italians. Likewise service occupations were passed down where families had specialized, e.g., barber, butler, soldier, clergyman, maidservant, policeman, farmer, merchant, etc.

The etymologists among you may relish the game of seeing who can name the most family names denoting occupation, e.g., Butler, Cook, Baker, Hunter, Fisher, Mason, Carpenter, Miller, Wright and Smith ("maker"), and such becoming obsolete names as Thatcher (former Prime Minister of Britain), one who thatched roofs with tree branches; Slater (ditto with slates); Fletcher (feathered arrows); Wheeler, Carter, Weaver (and Webster), Cooper (barrel-maker); Clark-Clerk—one whose livelihood depended on reading and writing; Arrowsmith (arrow-maker); etc. Those who made and sold kettles became known as Calderones in Italy, Calderons in Spain and Kessels in Germany and England. Kettle repairers were called Tinker in England and Cairds in Scotland. To cite 50 such names for your ancestral and present culture might be par for the course.

Females were prepared to be housewives, mothers and nurses. Such workers in providing life-supporting services enhanced family status in the pre-industrial community. By custom, unmarried males turned their salaries ("pay packet") over to their mother; husbands to their wives. Marriage was a vital family event. Prospective mates were chosen by the parents for potential contributions to the family welfare; romantic marriages were uncommon. Even today, marriages are arranged by East Indian and Chinese parents for their children. Divorce was sternly discouraged but a discrete liaison by the husband was condoned. Each family member strove to avoid formal affiliation with a member of a disreputable family. The family honor and name among the arrivals remained as worrisome as the reputation of a family-named business in the U.S.A. Commonly among immigrants, family wealth mattered less than name and reputation. To guard against scandal, a young single woman was scrupulously chaperoned. Children, as a matter of course, were expected to carry on the family customs of the old country.

After their arrival in the United States, many struggled, occupying low status in poorly paid menial jobs to support their families. Their goals were modest, by American standards: to own their own homes, perhaps even a small plot of garden but, above all, to provide their children with the advantages rigidly denied them.

As their children began to embrace the value system of the new culture, the immigrants became more or less aware that education need not be restricted, as in the old country, to traditional apprentice-ships—that the family in a modern industrialized society is much less needful of manual labor and peasant-style farmers; the need was for highly skilled mechanics, engineers, accountants, business managers, scientists, lawyers, teachers, professors in engineering and graduate schools who imparted professional skills. The apprenticeship system of the old world does not by itself prepare young people for work in the modern setting. This undervalues the knowledge or skill of a grandfather or father. Moreover, the high school diploma and college degree are indications of competence more or less accepted until proven otherwise. Such education, being costly, is likely to prolong the period of dependency on parents; that once trained and employed, offspring are less likely to return to the home base, but are rather more likely instead to establish their own household, understanding that social and job mobility can be crucial; that more often than not, demands of the job take at least short-term precedence over needs of the family; that even a marital disaster must not interfere with doing one's job; that American family patterns evidence an increasing drive toward prolonged job training and specialization; that family prestige is no longer uncritically equated with family name. The real flexibility of such patterns is a great puzzle or bewilderment of present American life.

The practice and pattern of insurance of the traditional family—gifts, loans without interest and other forms of help—can't compare with purchasable insurance. Here, one can buy insurance against theft, fire, earthquakes, hurricanes, catastrophic illness, with less onerous assurance that the help, however impersonal, will nonetheless be forthcoming, as in a modern hospital, especially in a teaching hospital.

Modern society causes the tightly knit "nuclear" family to be the dominant ideal, as opposed to the traditional extended or clannish family. Lack of desperate need of kin in times of trouble is one reason, thanks to such "safety nets" as social security, the need for which grew out of the tearing of the social fabric experienced in World War I, the Great Depression and World War II, and concomitant unprecedented educational opportunity and mobility afforded by the G.I. Bill of Rights for veterans.

The nuclear family also tends to shrink in modern society for reasons just intimated. Another reason is improved public health. Parents do not shape their lives to anticipate the likely loss of one or more children. As a result of the lessened intensity and diversity of interactions of the extended family, the nuclear family becomes more closely knit than had been the case in the era of the traditional and heavily patriarchal or matriarchal family.

Modern society also prizes independence. Young people therefore may seldom consult their parents on selecting a mate. They contrive their own dating. Resultant marriages may turn out to be happy liaisons—perhaps more so—than the parent-directed marriages. But the 50% divorce rate in some states, e.g., California and New York, argues that happiness is not easily won. Indeed, a new kind of composite family is evolving, as when a divorced wife with children marries a divorced man also with children. But modern society has an answer to that, too. One can cancel a marriage contract simply by signing a new contract *not* to be married.

B. Assignment #15

(1) Using the suggested list below, summarize—3 to 4 pages—how the cultural environment into which you were born influences your life and personality.

(2) Using the suggested list below, summarize—3 to 4 pages—how the cultural environment into which your mother/father was born influenced her/his life and personality.

(3) Ditto for grandparent.

SUGGESTED LIST*

ETHNICITY: Birthplace, prevailing political structure, Age at immigration to the U.S.A. Number of languages you speak? Read? Write?

HUMAN ENVIRONMENT: Urban? Suburban? Rural? Ethnic ghetto? Small town?

RACE: Negroid? Causasoid? Mongoloid? Mixed?

FAMILY SIZE: Number siblings who are older? Younger?

FAMILY COMPOSITION: Nuclear (with both parents) Extended? Are your parents divorced? How old were you then? Is a parent deceased? How old were you when it happened? Any step or half siblings? Describe family composition at present.

FAMILY RELIGION: Type of denomination, degree of involvement in religious observance—degree of influence your parents enforced on your beliefs—Sunday school attendance—amount of religious education? Influence on your family's religious persuasion and practices?

ECONOMIC STATUS: *Father's occupation*—tradesman, skilled laborer, mariner, professional, etc.? *Mother's occupation*—homemaker, professional?

How would you classify family's economic status: blue-collar, Middle class? Material possessions that reflect family's economic status? (no. cars, summer home, etc.) What advantages or disadvantages did you experience as a consequence of your family's economic status?

EDUCATIONAL STATUS: No. years schooling of father? Mother? Type of schooling of father? Mother? No. years schooling of self? Was formal education emphasized by parents? Influence of economic status on education? Aptitude, talents, skills, self-appraisal as a student— poorest subject, best subject? What sources of information do you rely

---

*Please exclude similar items which occur in the list of Open-ended questions.

on: radio, T.V. news, newspapers, magazines, lectures, non-fiction books? What type(s) of entertainment do you prefer: Sports, movies, T.V., theatre, concerts, dancing, biking, jogging, fiction novels, etc.?

STUDENT EXCERPTS

"Having lived most of my life in America, I've developed a different perspective on life as opposed to my parents and grandparents who came from the Phillippines. The dominant values given me by my American environment have been the pursuit of higher education and material accumulation. What seems to be lacking are ideas of sharing and helping others. My friends and acquaintances frequently remind me that 'you've got to look after yourself.'

"This creates a difficult conflict for me. While I'm taught by parents to care for my family, I'm also being coerced by the American culture to go out on my own and succeed. Sometimes I try not to let the desire for material wants underlie my goals but with the emphasis of such things by my peers, this seems impossible. In the Western culture, you're judged by what you own or what school you attend. I try to hang onto the values taught me by my parents and grandparents, but it's becoming increasingly hard. Someday I hope to have children; I hope to teach them about their Phillippine heritage, but without risk of creating a conflict in their home environment. Don't get me wrong. I'm grateful to be in this country. I just wish it didn't place such importance on material wealth and power."
R.E.

"I was born and lived in the Ukraine for the first 8 years of my life, and the last 11 in the U.S.A. Recently visitors from the Ukraine arrived and I was able to see how different their behavior and priorities are from ours. In the Ukranian culture everyone is very close. (I found it embarrassing when we went outdoors that my girl cousin wanted to hold hands.) Family is very important in the Ukraine. For example, when a couple marries they usually live for a while with the husband's parents. Ukranian family get-togethers are especially important during holidays. I'm often in conflict when my Americanized friends ask me to go skiing in Vermont during Christmas or to Florida during Spring vacation (Easter time). In the Ukraine church attendance is very important and one of the strongest bonds of the community.

"Women in the Ukranian culture do not have the same freedoms as they do in America. An unmarried woman in the Ukraine is considered an old maid, even a loose woman and looked upon badly. Once when I told my mother that I didn't want to get married but instead, I wanted to be like an American 'career woman,' she replied, 'Why? Are you going to start walking the streets?' Children are very important in the Ukraine where a typical family consists of 5 or 6 children. Here in America an Ukranian-American family consists of only 1 to 3 children. These and many other differences may change over time, but very slowly because the Ukraine is being industrialized." R.R.

"There is basically one great flaw in our American culture—too much focus on the individual, education and the economy to the neglect of the family. In this 'me first,' generation, we are being taught to push ourselves strictly for personal gain. I feel this especially leads to self-indulgence without any regard for those around us.

"Although Adam Smith's theory of the invisible hand states that 'those acting in their own self-interest will unintentionally benefit the society as a whole,' I feel that that leaves out those incapable of acting in their own self-interest, such as the poor and sick. With such a shallow view of life we are preventing ourselves from growing and putting limits on our capabilities as a people. If we had a more altruistic approach, it would benefit our society a lot more." P.P.

"This culture has taught me that the ideal person is a college graduate driven by a desire for money and power. In other words, 'the Wall Street type' like Donald Trump and Michael Milken. I feel I've been conditioned from the beginning to be overly competitive and never to accept anything but the best, including a large house and great material wealth. To be tall, slim and handsome, even if it means plastic surgery, are goals my friends and I seem to feel the need to strive for.

"Lacking are important considerations for artistic ability and spiritual values. I'm going to fight for these because they seem to me to be more important than the C.P.A., the M.B.A.'s and the disease of 'Yuppyitus.' " J.S.

"Almost on a par with competitiveness is the continual attempt to be creative. From day one in pre-school, I've been encouraged to be unique, be the one who comes up with the new idea. Even in history classes, I've been taught that our heroes are remembered for their implementation of a new idea or for being a unique individual.

"Evidence that supports our emphasis on creativity is that in recent years, schools and companies in other countries, notably Japan, are hiring Americans to teach their students and workers the 'American way' to promote creativity. We even idealize competitiveness in sports and my father, like most American fathers, has encouraged me to become proficient in one sport or another. In fact, sports as a profit-making form of entertainment exceeds that of any other country in the world." R.M.

a. Effects of Inherited Physical make-up, Cultural attributions &
   Self-perception

Female, male, tall, short, black, yellow, white, slim, stocky, strong,
frail, well-formed, deformed, gifted, handicapped—whichever of these
physical characteristics you may possess weren't your choice; they
were blueprinted in your genes. How come?

Over the centuries different humans lived in different environments.
As geneticists and physical anthropologists tell us, the pressure of
Darwinian natural selection accounts for the many different colors of
skin and eyes, shapes and size of facial features and body, as well as
differences in color and texture of hair. Eskimos, for example, are pale
with yellowish skin, poker straight black hair, slanting eyes with an
extra layer of skin called the epicanthic fold, and short arms and legs
in proportion to the torso. By contrast, The Watusi of East Africa are
black-skinned with frizzy hair, round eyes, and so long-limbed that the
average male is close to seven feet tall. A very active area of research
today concerns the underlying metabolic differences expressed in the
aforementioned obvious physical differences.

These physical differences occurred over thousands of years; the
different physical environments acting as the selective force for survival of each group. Consider the sustained cold of the arctic, for
example. Those mutations favoring survival enabled the Eskimo to
retain as much body heat as possible. Selection favored a compact
body with short limbs and minimal skin surface—less heat loss that
way. By contrast, the hot African environment of the Watusi required
efficient dissipation of body heat. Here the selection was for tall, slim
frames—more surface allowing better heat loss. The selective process
exerted by the environment may not mechanistically account for all
physical traits. One in particular is an extraordinarily large amount of
adipose (fatty) tissue in the upper thighs and buttocks of the Hottentot
Bushmen in Central Africa. This is known as *steatopygia,* but its origin
and purpose remain a mystery, except for the circumstance that they
are adapted to a rigorous desert. Here, too, is a hint of a metabolic
specialized trait: they can smell water from a long distance. Can we?

As humans developed tools, control over the environment bettered,
presumably subtly altering what was favored by natural selection. No
longer confined to one place, they could by intermarriage pass on their
favorable physical advantages with the result that—contrary to Adolph
Hitler's notion of a "pure master race"—all humans share a more-or-
less vast gene pool. (Only identical twins are identical!) Now, except

for differences in style of dress and bodily adornment, one's physical differences reflect centuries of interbreeding and genetic selection.

It is seductive for a culture to attribute greater value to one or more of the physical traits over others of its members. For example, most cultures have for centuries valued males more than females, presumably by such factors as fear of overpopulation; needs for warriors and farm laborers in face of the attrition of disease. Awareness of this situation was poignantly expressed by the actress Liv Ullman in opening her autobiography:[1]

> I was born in a small hospital in Tokyo. Mamma says she remembers two things; a mouse running across the floor which she took as a sign of good luck; a nurse bending down and whispering apologetically, 'I'm afraid it's a girl. Would you prefer to inform your husband yourself?'

Currently dominant North American cultures prize athletic and artistic talent; aggressive, competitive temperaments; high intellectual capacity; and tenacity and resourcefulness. Such preferences shape how an individual sees oneself as a member of that culture. Ideals erected during centuries of crowding emphasize community spirit and skillful control of aggression, e.g., the Japanese with their highly institutionalized forms of so called self-defense (T'ai Chi, Karate, Jujitsu). Some control or siphoning off or directing aggression gave rise to spectator sports in the Western World, e.g., baseball, football, hockey, prize-fighting. These and others enable the general public to redirect and thereby defuse hostility-induced tensions.

Ideals of physical beauty vary from culture to culture. One born with a tendency toward a corpulence that is highly prized by his culture is likely to perceive himself as superior. In a culture like the U.S.A. that puts a high premium on a lithe female body with largish breasts, a girl early inclined to plumpness may become so critically self-destructive as to either hide behind ever thicker layers of fat, or secretly practice starvation even to the current increase in the once-rare disease, anorexia nervosa, which can cause permanent damage, even death. Hence, accordingly, the increase in bulimia (bouts of gluttony). Likewise a non-aggressive person may develop a mania for muscle-building exercises or shrink from most social events.

In Western cultures that value tallness in males, a short-statured male born into a family with, say, three taller sisters may become even more self-conscious about lack of height and may endure lifetime

---

[1]Ullman, Liv *Changing* (New York: Knopf, 1989)

feelings of inadequacy and may, in popular parlance, compensate by becoming a "little Napoleon." People also differ in their birth position in the family: the youngest in a family of five siblings may be set in lifelong childish behavior.

One may speculate about Abraham Lincoln who had been perceived by his neighbors as a good boy who wasn't exactly lazy, "but his mind was often on books to the neglect of his work." But given his extraordinary qualities of intellect and leadership, joined with compassion, Lincoln may well have developed his perspective for humor mainly to offset attention from a high-pitched squeaky voice and a bony, ungainly physique often regarded as extremely ugly.

One born with an unusual physical feature or maimed by a serious illness, war wound or accident may fall prey to abrasive remarks. Small wonder that in the U.S.A. prosthetics and plastic surgery have become so important. Adulation of youth has made cosmetic surgery big business among the elderly. Anti-social—even criminal—behavior has proved in several instances to have stemmed from gross facial features inherited from birth. Cultural evaluations of one's physical endowments may also—obviously—affect choice of friends, sports, career, and popularity, thus providing a clue of sorts to origins of feelings of inferiority or superiority, arrogance or humility, defiance or tolerance. Also, inheritance of a strong physique with considerable innate energy may account for a happy, outgoing disposition as compared with the passive or phlegmatic behavior of one born with a sickly or frail constitution.

Several inherited conditions are not even remediable by modern plastic surgery or medical science. A case in point: a student whose parents had divorced when he was two; he'd had almost no contact at all with his father in the intervening years. This family history project prompted the student to interview his father. He'd been led to envision a quiet, shy man of average height whose sudden and unexpected bouts of rage had allegedly caused the divorce. During one of several interviews the student was astonished to learn that his paternal grandfather had been a dwarf. Embarrassments from childhood had led the student's father to defensiveness and irascibility, especially when anyone tried to get close. This revelation set the scene for better understanding between student and dad.

Such avenues to understanding may not demand sophisticated psychology. Aware or not, we are everlastingly observing, judging, and striving to understand, especially about family members. All some of us may know of them may be the slow accretion of understanding built up from casual, reserved daily interactions. Most humans in our dominant American culture, like icebergs, reveal only tips of themselves so to speak: most of their thoughts, experiences and sensitivities, especially painful ones, may remain submerged in a sea of daily wavelets. Only when we try to probe that silence may one discover how they regard themselves and others, and how they perceive others perceive them. Such feelings may be conveyed through words (much literature, especially murder mysteries, and drama depict eruption of violence as tiny pressures and insults accumulate to the point of unbearability), which brings us to the next assignment.

C. Assignment #16

The aim of this assignment is to help you arrive at better understanding of how family attributions influenced your self-perception. "Schnozola," "big-mouth," "runt," "peewee," "bean-pole," "long-stem," are among the more common attributions heard in families. Such attributions reflect cultural attitudes. It doesn't take much guesswork to trace the effect on one's self-image of one or more of these attributions which, when repeated often enough "stick" as a nickname.

Family proscriptions should also be considered, e.g. "Stop being a nuisance," "you're so bossy." "Everytime you open your mouth, you put your foot in it." "Can't you be trusted to do anything right?" Or, "You make me so proud," "How beautiful (or handsome) you are," "You were born under a lucky star," etc. Hearing these statements often enough in childhood, you may have begun taking them seriously and acting accordingly.

Looking into the mirror, try to recall such comments you say to yourself, or those made about you. The chart on the next page may stimulate recollection. After you've considered the possible influence of each on your self-perception, your next task is to:

(1) Describe—2 to 3 pages—how you see yourself and how you think others see you, emphasizing cultural determinants where recognized.

(2) Describe—2 to 3 pages—how you now surmise your parent sees her/himself, and how s/he thinks others see her/him, emphasizing cultural determinants where recognized.

(3) Ditto for grandparent.

SUGGESTED GUIDE TO DISCERNING INFLUENCES OF CULTURAL ATTRIBUTIONS ON SELF-PERCEPTION

Sex

- Is there a double standard in your home? Examples?
- Are you aware of sexual inequality in school? in employment?
- How do you feel about having been born a girl/boy?

Temperament

- Do you regard yourself as a relaxed person, easy to please?
- Are you short of patience? If you claim a mixture of the above two, largely dependent on circumstances, briefly explain.

Birthmarks

- Any so conspicuous as to make you self-conscious?

Height

- Which of the following describes your height: exceptionally tall, taller than average, average, short, much too short.

Posture

- Do you stand straight or stoop, or slouch?

Weight

- Would you call yourself: skinny, slim, average, plump or slightly overweight, heavy, fat?

Body-build

• Would you describe yourself as: shapely, plump, pudgy, stocky, muscular, athletic?

Distinguishing Endowments

• Unusually big hands, ears, feet; bowlegs; atrophied limb; hunchbacked?

Energy level

• Unusually high, mostly high, average, mostly low, unusually low?

Face shape

• Square, oval, round, heart-shaped, pointed chin, cleft or dimpled chin, heavy jowelled, high cheekbones, cheek dimpled, flat, fleshy, beautiful, plain, mousy?

Brows

• thin, straight, arched, bushy?

Eyes

• (size & shape) round, small, almond-shaped, bulging, deepset or hooded, large? (color) green ("hazel"), black, brown, grey, heavily bespectacled?

Skin

• (condition & color) smooth, acneed, corrugated, pock-marked, ruddy, pale, rosy, sallow, pasty, brown, dark-brown, mahogany, yellowish ("olive"), "wheat colored" (Japanese)?

Nose

• Aquiline, retrousse, small, bulbous, well-formed, pointed, flat, hooked, flared nares, pug, bony?

Lips

• full, thin, pursed, puckered, prominent, thick?

Age

• adult, middle-aged, youthful, old, doddering, spry, feeble, vigorous, lazy, sluggish?

Teeth

• regular, irregular, bucktoothed, normal over-bite, undershot jaw, yellow-stained, gap-toothed, noticeably false?

Hair

• (Texture) thin, thick, straight, frizzy, wispy, wiry?
(Color) red, brown, black, auburn, gray, sun-bleached or streaky, white, toupe, wig?
(Style) close-cropped, Afro-shaved, pony-tail, tight bun, braided, poker-straight, bangs, chignon, kinky, permanented, curly?

Acquired Abnormality

• broken-nose, limping walk (from accident or disease—diabetes, war-injury)?

General Health

• Good, poor, sickly, unusually good, long-lived, asthmatic, weak, billious?

Excerpts from former students on self-perception.

I'm 18 years-old and come from a fairly traditional Italian family. I'm 5′7½″ tall, average weight, but I'd like to lose about 15 pounds. I wear a 9½ shoe, have hazel eyes with brown specks and rather long lashes. My hair is naturally curly and dark brown. I don't like wearing glasses because they detract from my appearance, which is not beautiful in the first place. I don't like my nose because it's large like my mother's, but I do like my long nails. Many are amazed that I can keep them so long without breaking. The compliment and attention I get on my nails makes me want to keep them extra long. I guess that means I like attention and to provoke responses in others. E.I.

On the whole I'm fairly happy with my appearance but if there was one thing I could change it would be my legs. I think they are shapeless and bony and not very feminine. N.M.

In the past I was preoccupied with my physical appearance and what people thought of it. Now my attitude has changed. I realized through this assignment that there was much about me that I didn't know and needed to discover. Hence, I started focusing on the factors that made me what I am, how I feel and why. Each new discovery has contributed to greater self-confidence. A.M.

The first thing people notice about me is my eyes; they're brown and almond-shaped. People tell me that I have a very deep look and that sometimes I don't even need to talk because my eyes will do the talking. I have the same smile as my father. As a child I had to wear braces and am thankful to have straight beautiful teeth. My skin tone is pretty dark. I don't like my hair: it is straight, dark, very thin and never stays the way I want it. I'm short, 5'3" and it bothers me because a lot of people make fun of me. I think I see myself more clearly after trying to describe myself. E.L.

Excerpts from interviews with parent re. her/his self-perception and experiences with how others perceived her/him.

MOTHER

My mother sees herself as one who has not been a great success in life. The traumatic experiences of being brought up in a broken home and living in poverty has made her bitter. She says she tries to cover up these feelings, but from time-to-time, she can't. Nevertheless, she says she forces herself to accept life as it is, not as she would have liked it to have been.

She reports that others see her as quite different. They regard her as one who is well-read, well-traveled, intelligent, opinionated and self-confident. People have also told her that she is physically attractive, although she doesn't agree. She doesn't like herself much physically. People have also told her that she's individualistic, self-confident and a great success at rearing her children. C.W.

My mother thinks she is too critical of herself and others. She knows that she has a great capacity to love others and would give her life for her family. She watches her diet, exercises and takes pride in her appearance. She is very knowledgeable and intelligent, pushes herself beyond her limits and is, at times, exhausted.

Others told her that they perceive her as gentle, kind, smart, determined, always busy. She works and takes college courses at night in preparation for a teaching career. They have also told her that she is logical and calculating. J.M.

My mother was very uncomfortable talking about herself. Basically, she's unhappy with her weight. She feels that her life is boring. She's very hard working (which is true). She feels that her life would have been very different and possibly better, if she hadn't married.

People say that my mother works too hard, that she's a good woman who jokes a lot, and they say that she's beautiful, despite her argument about her weight. R.R.

My mother considers herself a snob and is not happy about it. She also thinks she's smart and capable of accomplishing anything. She's open to other's feelings and ideas and considers herself well-rounded. She says she's an intellectual, a pseudopsychologist and a well-read woman with a positive and strong self-image.

Others have told her that she's funny and joyful, well-read, intelligent and a great cook. Also, she is trustworthy, caring and loving. I agree and think she's afraid of no one or any situation. D.A.

FATHER:

"After 40 years of steady employment, I've grown to know little else beside the job, family and a few small relaxations. I find it hard to believe that in a short while, I'll be a senior citizen. Both my sons make me proud, but sometimes I worry about them. I guess most parents are that way. I just want them to have the opportunities to make the best choices they can.

"I don't think much about how others view me. I do what has to be done and try not to hurt anyone; it's that simple. I really don't see why anyone would think anything unusual about me." R.A.M.

My father sees himself as a career man, a lawyer, good-looking, confident, enjoys family time, especially with his own family at home. This is a quality that he feels has been passed down by his own father, an overwhelming love of children and a desire to make life easier for them than it was for himself. He is always trying to better himself and says, I work hard so that my children won't have to.

I see myself in him, as do my brothers, and that makes us very happy. People have said that my father is the best kind of father a son could want. He's kind, caring and a good-provider. R.M.

My father and I have as many things in common as we have differences. He, too, is short, about 5'2" and weighs 160 pounds. He's 74 years old. I think that's only a few years younger than my grandfather. Because of a stroke, my father walks with a cane. There are few things in life he seems to care for, but he does want me and my sister to finish college. He'd be just as content with a 13" black-and-white T.V. as with a 30" colored one.

People see him as a sweet old man, a hard worker who cares very much for his family, and who would never lie or cheat people. D.H.

My father looks very much like me, except that he's luckier to be somewhat taller than me. My guess is that he dreamed of becoming a professional quarterback because ever since I was 10, he has made me join football teams hoping that I could someday quarter-back the Jets to the superbowl title, thus vicariously fulfilling his dream. Needless to say, he was disappointed that I didn't grow to 6'5", but I think he's over that and accepts the fact that I want to become a Certified Public Accountant. He's generous, very opinionated which often makes our discussions end up in an argument. He's also very competitive, hates to lose. All in all, most people think he's not that bad for a man his age. J.S.

MATERNAL GRANDMOTHER

My grandmother is 5'3" tall and extremely thin. Her eyes are brown and although now white, her hair was also once brown and wavy. At age 15, both her parents died and she was left to care for six younger brothers and sisters, the youngest of which was only 1. At 16, she married a farmer and raised her siblings as well as more children of her own.

She is now ill and sees herself as a very caring and giving person. There are times when she lets her anger explode and she strikes out. Then she feels so confused that she won't talk to the person who made her angry for days. She knows she's stubborn and has secret favorites among her children, although she's a firm believer in family closeness.

Others, especially her children, see her as a tyrant, a ruler supreme, and an angry person who thinks she's always right and a no-nonsense person. M.R.

PATERNAL GRANDFATHER

In response to my question, my grandfather said, I'm quite happy. I've lived a long, decent life, have a family I love greatly. I'm not claiming to be perfect since I've made more than my share of mistakes. I don't think a person is really alive if he's constantly trying to avoid his problems. I believe that a person's personality adds up to all the decisions s/he has had to make in life. I sometimes feel that I'm being overbearing and rude, but people who really know me tell me that I'm not always like that. They say that they regard me as just an average guy who gets along with most people because I never ask for too much of anyone. T.M.

My grandfather sees himself as one who has accomplished a lot in life. He grew up having to fend for himself and his younger brother. He fought in 5 star battles in World War II, and says he feels lucky that he came out unscathed. He feels he has done the most with his life, married, brought up 4 successful children.

Others have told my father that they see him as a trustworthy person, loyal and always there when you need him. They say he's a great and handsome man, and I fully agree! P.Q.

b. Effects Of Decisive and Crucial Life Experiences

We live by growth and change, some effected by conscious decision, some by happenstance—each a turning point—triggered perhaps by advice from a teacher, parent, book passage, film, accident, sudden windfall, urgent need or a move to another country, town, a promotion, marriage, new acquaintance—in short—as many other experiences as one thinks it changed attitudes, behavior and goal.

Jane Addams for example recalled that it was the dehumanizing poverty in London's East End that had made her become a settlement worker.

Helen Keller tells how her life as a blind, deaf mute was transformed when she met her young teacher, Anne Sullivan, who was also partly blind. Keller finally had "seen light in darkness, . . . heard through the barriers of deafness and . . . broke the silence with her own voice."

Another actuality: Michel Cojot discovered when adult that he was Jewish; that his true name was Goldberg. It led him to abandon wife and career to search for information about his father. He eventually comes face-to-face with his father's Nazi murderer and, toward the end of his odyssey, Michel comes to know not only about his father, but to understand himself.

Examples abound, including those you will find at the end of this section which were excerpted from accounts by former students. It's your turn.

D. Assignment #17

(1) Describe a decision or experience which crucially changed your life.

(2) Describe a decision or experience which crucially changed your mother's/father's life.

(3) Ditto for your maternal grandmother/paternal grandfather.

Some excerpts from students about decisive and crucial life experiences.

"During my high school years, I rarely traveled more than three miles from home which is in a mainly Jewish and Italian suburb. I worked part-time at a local wall paper store and the Hallmark shop. Then came college. It opened up a new world: for the first time I met students and professors from all over the world.

"I now work for an international firm in Manhattan. Commuting everyday to New York City has enabled me to see my first Broadway show, visit several museums, sample Japanese, Russian and Indian foods, etc. That decision to attend college has (made) me a better rounded person." C.W.

"I was born and brought up in New York City and always loved its hundreds of restaurants, nightclubs, museums, parks, shops and different cultures from all over the world. Then last month, my uncle was murdered by a gang of teenagers, none of whom is more than 16 years old.

"My uncle was a hard-working family man who also loved the city. Now I feel nothing but hatred and disgust for it. All the aspects that I once loved about it are dead. After 21 years of life here, I want desperately to get away. I want a place where drugs don't rule people's behavior, and where people care for human life." D.A.

"A week before my high school graduation, doctors found a tumor in my calf. After six weeks of chemotherapy they operated and removed the tumor, after which came six weeks of radiation therapy. This experience made me question my mortality and God's motive, perhaps, for punishing me or trying to teach me something. I reviewed the seventeen years since my birth to see if I had already fulfilled my purpose and that therefore, it was time for me to go.

"After I seemed to be cured, I began listing things I wanted to accomplish. I assumed God was giving me time not only to achieve these goals, but to repent for my sins and prepare my soul for Judgement. This is where I am now. I appreciate life more and try to be with my family and listen to them more carefully." R.R.

"One event that turned my life around 360°. That was in the 6th grade when I became friends with Anthony. I think it was because we two were the only non-whites in the entire school. We were never really picked on since we knew martial arts, but we both felt like driftwood in a vast, empty ocean, because we were treated like outcasts.

"For a while I tried to be like the white kids, but Anthony pointed out to me that you have to be yourself, and that if others don't like you for being yourself—then screw them. It took Anthony, a true friend, to make me feel proud of being just me and I'll never forget him for that." D.H.

"[My] . . . most influential change began when my father retired after 25 years on the police force and he and my mother bought property overseas to live there. Since I wanted to continue my undergraduate education at Pace, I moved in with my brother, who is also unmarried . . .

"From that point on, my life changed. I now have to buy and cook my own food, take care of my own laundry and even get a higher paying job which meant increasing my weekly work hours. In other words, I'm learning to be responsible for myself. It has put me on the go at all times, but after seven months, I feel that I'm successfully meeting the challenge." L.L.

"September 6, 1988 was the first day of my fast. For 90 days thereafter my daily diet consisted of nothing more than water and 5 Optifast shakes. The first pain I experienced was psychological. Until you are denied food, or deny yourself of it, you may never realize quite how much of life revolves around food. Every social gathering seems to include some type of refreshment, and time and again, I felt excluded as I watched my friends stuff their faces during my 90-day fast.

"The second type of pain I suffered was physical. After 2½ weeks I landed in the hospital; it turned out that I was allergic to Optifast. Nevertheless, I was so determined to lose weight that I continued fasting for 2½ months more. Although many of my bodily functions were affected by this diet, heart, breathing, digestion and menstruation, I never let up.

"However, when I lost the excess weight, my whole life changed. Not only did the way people perceive me change, but so, too, did the way I perceive myself. For a while I felt very vulnerable. I had spent the past 18½ years building a wall around myself for fear of being hurt. I realized that rather than protect me, this wall had hurt me, that true happiness comes from within and from inner contentment with self.

"I shall never again allow myself to gain back that 'wall' of weight and feel stronger in the knowledge that when something is important to me, I can have total control over my behavior." J.M.

"As a result of this experience my entire life changed. It goes back 3 years when, as a junior in the top 10 in my class, I was given a choice of electives. Since I wanted an easy course, I chose Accounting even though, like the rest of the boys in my school, I looked down on all business courses.

"Halfway through the first quarter of the term, the teacher began challenging me with afterschool assignments. Also after class, he would often show me the basics of all areas of business. By the end of that term, I was amazed to discover that not only had I learned to like business, but that I was especially good in it. This led me to decide to work toward a B.A. in Accounting at Pace University and then later, if all goes well, to work for a C.P.A. And it was all due to the influence of one teacher to whom I will be eternally grateful." R.M.

Chapter Seven

Putting It Together

Bringing this undertaking to its conclusion is perhaps the most enlightening gain from your efforts. Now to integrating all or big portions of your summaries, questionnaires, notes (including photos), into an autobiography of sorts showing how certain previously vague forces and past events shaped family patterns and that unavoidably shaped your life, and its code of values.

How to Begin

Scan your looseleaf notes, summaries, completed assignments and other folder materials. Label all photos (or copies) which you propose to include in your final report—faces, places, dates and occasion for each photo. Those who have taped interviews may now wish to transcribe them. A suggested time-saver is simply to replay the tape(s) when needed and then preserve them as a family memento.

There are several ways to begin writing. A short paragraph on the origin and extent of use of your surname is one possible choice. Or you might sketch a childhood experience, crucial family crisis, memorable historical event or an apt literary quotation. See whether you can set a tone attractive to your reader.

Where to Begin

Historians often start with a point in the past and move forward. It better enables them to comprehend historical change, since it follows a logical sequence of events. I'd recommend beginning with yourself as you are now. Such a personal interest in analyzing historical material is apt to be especially attractive and a good way to get over initial obstacles and—as explained later—it may appeal to the reader as well. It's also consistent with the practice encouraged by previous assignments: to look at life objectively, be it one's own, one's parent, grandparent, or anyone else's, and from such angles as: era of birth, the effect of the environment (physical and cultural) on one's inherited characteristics which helped shape one's values, outlook and self-perception.

Write—But Coherently—As You Talk

As noted (Ch. 2, Assignment #3: Review of The Literature), especially interesting autobiographies were those—by definition—written in the first person: they're generally less formal, less apt to sound like a perfunctory job. Also it makes it easier for you to examine and express your deeper feelings and opinions about experiences and people. Imagine that you're addressing a close sibling, friend or even a yet-unborn family member. St. Augustine found it easiest to address his autobiographical confessions to God.

If use of the first person "I" makes you feel hesitant, write impersonally—as if about somebody else. It may even enable you to become more objective, but whichever approach you choose, try to maintain a natural, almost conversational tone. Where possible paint word pictures, e.g., ("My paternal grandfather was slim and tall as a telephone pole," or, "My mother's complexion was like a Dresden doll's").

Statement of Purpose

Harry S. Truman's opening statement of purpose for his autobiography was to show how a country boy grew up to become a respected U.S.A. president. The novelist Ellen Glascow promised an "honest portrayal of an interior world." Russell Baker's aim was to show how the past shapes the future; Michel Cajot's intent was to define his own identity. Similar examples abound. In fact, the very title of your Guidebook suggests a statement of purpose—to see yourself as history, part of your family history spanning three generations. As discovered earlier in your assignment on Review of The Literature

(Ch. 2, #3), a statement of purpose up front is likely to contribute to a more cohesive, and successful autobiography.

Additional Suggestions

Let your ideas settle: don't expect to write the whole thing in one sitting. Use your Detailed Guidesheet to refer to each category in turn. When you can't seem to think of a transition from one period of time to another, do something else. A practice that has paid off for me is carrying a small pad to jot down an unexpected idea or thought.

Plan a linear development of your story from birth to now. Events may group into stages, e.g., early childhood; birth of other siblings; early school years; first experience (skating, biking, camping); how your family celebrated holidays; how you and your siblings got along; what you enjoyed most as a child, etc. These events are frequently memorialized with photographs. Use these photos liberally as focal points.

Each stage—childhood, adolescence, young adult—admixes the good and bad, sad and happy. All relate somehow to family, friends, pets, toys, fantasies, schooling, books, play, insights and disillusionment. Tell about these as you see them now and where they do or don't share your present value system, and how you judge and trust they may have helped your growth and wisdom. Include mention of what you may have missed: perhaps a grandparent who died too soon; no room of your own; not learning a wanted skill, etc. For any stage in your life, mention any turning point and try to analyze why it changed your life and thinking.

Where possible associate a personal event or experience with an historical event. Where you may write, for example:

"I was born on July 10th, 1969, in Garden City, N.Y.," try this:

"On the day I was born—July 10, 1969—my father said that our country hit the moon. What he meant was that that was the day when our U.S. astronauts were the first humans to land on the moon."

Certain experiences may be associated with a particular occasion or period in life which may have induced behavior change. Compare these two versions of the same event:

"In May, 1986, I was graduated from Polander High School in Hazelton, Pennsylvania."

or

"For my graduation from Polander High School—May, 1968—Hazelton, Pennsylvania, my parents gave me a gift that I shall cherish—an 8 string guitar. I spent every minute I could learning to play it so that I could memorize all the chords. My skill improved to band. Now my weekend gigs help pay my tuition. I don't think I'll ever give up this activity."

Next take up the completed Detailed Guidesheet for your parent and proceed in the same manner. When you feel you've accounted for the questions in each of the categories, go on and do the same for maternal/paternal grandparent. Remember: a photo of you and your parent or grandparent may serve as a good focal point for bringing in additional relevant information about him/her, and drawing comparisons between the two of you as representatives of your respective generations.

Lay the 3 Detailed Guidesheets side-by-side and compare the answers in each category, i.e., for yourself, parent and grandparent. Note here the differences, if any, re. birth order, number of siblings, physical and cultural environments, number of years of formal education, and so on, up to and including the last category. Again, a photo may serve as a good focal point for bringing in other information about her/him, and drawing comparisons among you.

In drawing comparisons do comment on close parallels among the generations as well as divergences. How was your grandmother's awareness of being a woman affected by the male reactions and general attitudes toward women in her day? And what about your mother's reaction as compared with *her* mother's and your own? Most people harbor a single, emotional composite memory of their childhood, youth, etc. Reality mixes bad and good, happiness and misery. Let yourself consider these and express them as the urge seizes you. It should help your reader to empathize more warmly and will provide you with a basis for recognizing possible changes in values.

These synthesizing post-analyses can be made to fit in less awkwardly as you trace your progress from your earliest years. Your aim—in sum—is to see your life clearly where you interacted and interpreted places, family members and events. Many of the summaries from assignments you've already completed are likely to ease your efforts. Keep going back to them with various questions about how they may serve at a particular point in your account.

Strive as much as possible to be specific. A statement like the following is too vague, failing to characterize the type of conflicts and to include examples:

"There have been many conflicts in my generation."

Now compare it with this statement:

"There have been many military conflicts in my generation, namely, Grenada, Panama and, most recently, Iraq (1991). However, my generation also produced . . . etc."

When you have brought your autobiography to the present, reread it for other insertions that may occur to you re., for example, technological, cultural and medical advances achieved in each lifetime, major historical events and issues, etc. Also proofread to correct sentence structure, typos, spelling and legibility of print.

Use the cover provided in this guidebook to enhance your presentation.

Your autobiography is likely, then, to include reminiscences, reflections and feelings about specific experiences and people—in effect become a memoir of maturing and learning.

Personal Reactions

For the benefit of family members and friends who may have contributed to your effort, and for your future readers, conclude with mention of what you've learned about your family that you did not know before starting on this project, and what it has meant to you.

Some student excerpts

"This project has revealed more about my mother's youthful days than I ever imagined possible. My mother was such a lively, spirited young woman who enjoyed sports, was very outgoing until she married. The mother I now have, though much older, is very serious, private and not as outgoing as I would like her to be." R.O.

"This project has given me the opportunity to think about my family. I had never wanted to know much about them other than what was on the outside. Now that I've learned some things, I ask even more questions that I never before thought to ask." J.S.

"I discovered a lot of things that my grandmother and I have in common. We also have a lot of the same reactions to certain situations. The way she brought up my mother enabled me to see a lot of my mother in her, and me in my mother." M.S.

"Delving into my family history has been like opening a Pandora's box. I have become more curious about family incidents and intend to work on this more as the years go by." A.D.

"I learned how much alike my grandmother, mother and I are. It's quite scary to see the similarities that I never realized before. For example, we are all savers, always banking on a possible use of something to avoid throwing it away. It's a horrible habit, but one I feel I may have been helpless to avoid." A.D.F.

Check Points for Your Final Draft

1. A *title page* listing *your name, name and course number, date, instructor's name, name of your school;*

2. Second page containing a short paragraph granting your instructor permission to include a copy of your family history in the school's records, and to use same for whatever scholarly purposes it may serve in future—(this is at the discretion of your teacher);

3. *Number* on each page of your manuscript and approximately 1½ inch margins on four sides;

4. *Legibly* dark typescript or handwriting—*doublespaced;*

5. A Table Of Contents (optional);

6. Proper footnotes and an index in the back;

7. A bibliography;

8. Secure mounting of photos;

9. Insertion of your work-sheets and Detailed Guidesheets at the end of your manuscript (at discretion of your teacher).

Here is a world map on which students can plot where they and their families came from.

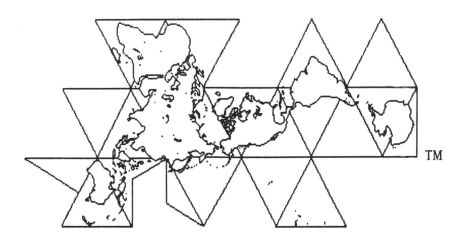

TM

My Family History
Through Three Generations

Class _____

Teacher _____

Date _____

Family Photos